Sharie King Hebrews 10:39

PRAISE FOR
I LOVE YOU MORE
(EXCEPT WHEN I DON'T)

"What a challenging and encouraging book! This is just what every woman needs to hear. You don't have to feel shame when you feel like your love for Jesus loses out to all the other responsibilities in your life. He understands how we can feel overwhelmed, discouraged and disappointed. This book reminds us that all He ever wants for us is a relationship."

DERWIN AND VICKI GRAY
Lead Pastor and Executive Director of
Transformation Church

"Sharie King has told the truth in an honest, sometimes comfortable (and sometimes not), compelling, and readable style. Frankly, there is something here for everyone. She writes with vulnerability, avoids clichés and platitudes, and seamlessly weaves the biblical story in and out of her own life story as an injured young girl, aspiring wife, caring mother, honest friend, and recovering perfectionist."

ROBERT W. CANOY
Dean and Professor of Christian Theology,
Gardner-Webb University, School of Divinity

"Sharie offers profound wisdom, heartfelt grace, and solid biblical teaching with warmth and wit! As a woman who longs to love Jesus more, I was both deeply encouraged and convicted by this book. *I Love You More* is on the top of my recommended reading list for Christian women seeking to deepen their relationship with Jesus Christ."

MARIAN JORDAN ELLIS
Author of *Stand* and Founder of
Redeemed Girl Ministries

"There are two things I look for in every book I read: honesty and words that point me to Jesus. Sharie King has given me both in the beautiful and truth-filled, *I Love You More*. As a woman who wants to love God more than anything else, the words in this book touch a deep place in my heart and pave a clear path for me to follow as I maneuver the busy road of life. Thank you, Sharie. May this book turn all of us to look back full into the face of our greatest love, Jesus."

LISA WHITTLE
Speaker and Author of *I Want God*
and *Put Your Warrior Boots On*

"No matter what season you are in, this book will encourage you to keep going. Sharie's realness and vulnerability

paired with God's truth pulls you in and allows you to
see the circumstances in your own life through the lens of
hope. I know this book will challenge you and encourage
you to fall in love with Jesus over and over again."

HOLLY MYERS

Pastor's Wife at Revolution Church and
Speaker with Clayton King Ministries

"As a professional counselor, I am always looking for re-
sources to give to my clients that could possibly help them
heal and move past whatever is causing them to remain
stuck in life. I'm thankful to have found another resource
in this powerful and encouraging book by Sharie King. I
believe Sharie's personal story, combined with her words
of wisdom founded in Scripture will propel many into a
deeper and better relationship with Jesus, the Ultimate
Counselor."

ZACHARY DICKSON, M.A., LPC-I,

Founder of Hopetown LLC

"Whew! Overwhelmed, discouraged, or anxious about
managing all the responsibilities you're juggling while
also trying to make time for Jesus? Whether your career
is household manager or one outside of the home, you
will want to keep Sharie King's *I Love You More* as a go-to
for many years. You'll be able to easily relate to her trans-

parent stories, and you'll treasure her encouraging advice on how to have the relationship that Christ desires us to have with Him. You'll be drawn into this book from the first page!

SHARON WEBB, PHD, LPCS, NCC
Associate Professor of Psychology & Counseling;
Human Services Program Coordinator
Gardner-Webb University

I LOVE YOU
MORE

(except when I don't)

FIGHTING TO KEEP JESUS FIRST

Sharie King

Fedd Books
P.O. Box 341973
Austin, TX 78734
www.thefeddagency.com

Published in association with The Fedd Agency, Inc., a literary agency.

ISBN: 978-1-943217-63-2
eISBN: 978-1-943217-64-9

Printed in the United States of America
First Edition 15 14 13 10 09 / 10 9 8 7 6 5 4 3 2

To Clayton, Jacob, and Joseph.
I am so proud of the men of God you are becoming.
Thank you for loving me more.

TABLE OF CONTENTS

INTRODUCTION..13

1. I LOVE YOU MORE THAN MYSELF.............................19

2. I LOVE YOU MORE WITH MY PAST...........................39

3. I LOVE YOU MORE THAN MY PERFECTION.....................61

4. I LOVE YOU MORE THAN MY POSITION.......................87

5. I LOVE YOU MORE THAN MY DISAPPOINTMENT................111

6. I LOVE YOU MORE IN MY FORGIVENESS.....................129

7. I LOVE YOU MORE THAN MY DREAMS........................153

8. I LOVE YOU MORE IN MY COMMUNITY.......................173

9. I LOVE YOU MORE WITH MY FUTURE........................189

CONCLUSION...209

ENDNOTES...213

ACKNOWLEDGMENTS..217

INTRODUCTION

The day is finally over! My hand grabs the last glass from the sink and places it in the dishwasher. If I can only muster enough energy to scoop the dry soap, close the dishwasher door, and push the start button, I will be free—free to shed my shoes and plop down on that couch that's calling my name.

I'm finally horizontal. My feet are up on the ottoman, and my head is resting on my comfy couch pillow. My heavy eyelids start to close, but my two boys' loud cheers (along with my FOMO) startle me awake for the football replay. Why am I torturing myself? Just let go.

I start to drift again when the irresistible voice of my youngest son steals away any opportunity to rest. "Mama. Cuddle?"

I know what you're thinking. "Aw, he's so sweet." You're right. He is sweet, and I know this cute stage won't be around forever, but what you don't know is that we cuddle differently. I like to snuggle until we drift off to sleep. When he asks to cuddle, what he means is, "Will you scratch my back until I fall asleep?" Sharie, the worn-out human being, is frustrated. But Sharie, the mom, wonders how many moments like this she has left before this guy becomes too embarrassed to crave her affection.

Guilt-love takes over. Guilt-love is that emotion every mom feels rising from her gut when that sweet voice and those tender eyes tempt her to smother her child with love. We convince ourselves that our children need us, but honestly, we're the ones who can't resist feeling loved. My body taps into energy reserves unknown to me as I lift my arm to the official scratching position and commence my motherly duty. I don't know how I will last, but here goes nothing.

An hour later, I wake up in a panic. "Guys, it's bedtime!"

"Will you tuck me in?"

My groggy mind argues, "Seriously? No way! Tuck yourself in."

But again, his clear blue eyes and adorable freckles cast a spell on me, and I find myself standing in his dark room dazed and waiting for Joseph to obey our two-minute toothbrush rule. I'll wait for this, but I'm *not* climbing up to that top bunk.

I try to snag a hug and kiss before he reaches his ladder, but he sneaks past me and climbs under the covers wearing a sneaky grin. Sharie, the human being, is irritated, but Sharie, the mom, is giggling inside! I guess he gets a full-service tuck-in tonight. I force myself to love him more than my sleep. I climb the ladder, hug his little neck, kiss his freckled cheek, and speak these words to his soul, "I love you, and I'm proud of the man of God you're becoming." Descending the ladder, his tender voice responds, "I love you more!"

It's the first time he's ever said it. I'm already in the hallway when I process his words, and my eyes begin to leak tears. I can hardly breathe as a flood of warm love flows down my throat settling in my heart. I realize that I almost missed this moment. His innocent confession keeps circling through my mind, "I love you more." I want to hear it. I need to hear it.

When I was lying on the couch, every part of me wanted to resist guilt-love. I was more in love with my sleep than my priceless son on this monumental night. I didn't want to scratch, or wait as he brushed his teeth, or climb the bunk-bed ladder. I didn't want to love Joseph more, but mom-guilt made me.

The first time Joseph told me he loved me more, my heart melted. But the second time, I thought, *Wait. I birthed this kid. He can't possibly love me more.* So I argued back, "No, I love *you* more." Now we argue about who loves who more on a regular basis. It's become a silly family argument because we know there's no real way to measure our love, but we want to try to outdo each other anyway.

That story is sweet and heartwarming, but let me share a not-so-sweet story. My son, Jacob, woke up one morning thinking disobedience was the word of the day. He had a hard time conceding to any of my wishes, and I reacted. "If you really love me, you'll obey. Stop saying you're sorry, and start obeying me." I know. I was harsh, and his deflated face brought on the Lord's conviction. Jesus asked me, "Sharie, do you love me?"

"Yes, Lord!"

"Do you always obey me?"

"No."

I soon wore the same deflated face as Jacob and initiated a repentant conversation with my seven-year-old son. Humbling.

As the Father has loved me, so have I loved you. Now remain in my love. If you keep my commands, you will remain in my love, just as I have kept my Father's commands and remain in his love. I have told you this so that my joy may be in you and that your joy may be complete. My command is this: Love each other as I have loved you. Greater love has no one than this: to lay down one's life for one's friends. You are my friends if you do what I command. I no longer call you servants, because a servant does not know his master's business. Instead, I have called you friends, for everything that I learned from my Father I have made known to you. You did not choose me, but I chose you and appointed you so that you might go and bear—fruit that will last—and so that whatever you ask in my name the Father will give you. This is my command: Love each other. (John 15:9-17)

Have these verses ever scared or intimidated you? If we don't keep his commands, will he still love us? Will he still consider us his friends? Have you ever felt like a failure loving Jesus? Have you ever wondered how to make yourself love Jesus more?

Me too. If we were standing face-to-face, you might assume this pastor's wife has it all together. But if we sat down to talk, I'd confess how hard it is for me to love Jesus more than myself. He's so perfect. I'm so not. He's so God. I'm so—*definitely*—not. Still, these facts don't eliminate my yearning to love Jesus more or how incapable I feel trying. I know Jesus deserves all my love. I bet you do too. My soul wants to live in the safety of his love and favor, so why don't my actions match my desire? Why do we struggle to love Jesus more?

Take another look at the end of John 15. "I have called you friends, for everything that I learned from my Father I have made known to you. You did not choose me, but I chose you and appointed you so that you might go and bear fruit—

> HAVE YOU EVER WONDERED HOW TO MAKE YOURSELF LOVE JESUS MORE?

fruit that will last—and so that whatever you ask in my name the Father will give you" (John 15:15-16).

If you share my frustration of wanting to love Jesus more, perhaps you also want to share my journey of discovering how you can. Jesus will teach us everything we need to know to become who he's designed us to be. "A person can receive only what is given them from heaven" (John 3:27). So I'm praying that this book is the Lord's way of taking you on a journey to love Jesus more than you do today. Let's let Jesus transform us together.

CHAPTER 1

I Love You More Than Myself

"How many of you have said, 'This is going to kill me,' and yet here you sit?"
—Luci Swindoll, Women of Faith Conference

THE HELMET

I hug every curve as I drive from my home in the North Carolina mountains to my boyfriend in the foothills. Finally, after two-and-a-half hours, I pull into his driveway, thankful we can finally have a conversation without worrying about a long-distance phone bill. He runs from his front door, hops in my car, and takes me to a Mexican restaurant.

Life is perfect until we take our seats, and he puts a cinched shopping bag in front of me. "I have something for you!"

I'm not excited, but I know I should be. He is filled

with enthusiasm while I'm full of girlfriend guilt. I force a smile, but I want to throw up. Why didn't I get him a gift? Oh, that's right. I'm a rock-climbing guide living below the poverty level.

I reach for the bag, simultaneously offering my heart a pep talk: "Sharie, think about something happy and fake it!" When my hands find a super-expensive rock-climbing helmet, all I can think is, "Great! How am I going to pay him back for this? Clean his house? Do his laundry? Cut his lawn?" Mandolin music tries to boost my spirit, but I don't play along. My guilt meter is registering *mortified* as Clayton stares into my eyes.

"Why did you get me this?"

Oblivious, he candidly answers, "Because I care about you, and I don't want you to die."

He's proud of himself, and he should be. He's relishing this moment while I'm resenting him for it. What's wrong with me? A small part of me senses that I'm broken, but I don't want to ruin our young love. I like to feel my heart pitter-patter and the butterflies in my stomach. I don't want to lose my blissful love lens. So I sip my soda, hoping it will wash away my deficiency.

Two years later, I still haven't addressed this broken part of me. I don't feel it as I saunter down the steps of a plantation house in my glowing white gown. My love doesn't feel deficient staring into my future husband's weepy eyes as we profess undying love beneath a grove of oak trees. My love feels more than sufficient driving to our honeymoon, cheeks aching from that wedding per-ma-smile. But riding down the road five years later, I hear myself confess, "Clayton, do you realize it's taken me seven years of you loving me for me to believe that I don't have to earn it? I've made a decision to accept that you love me for me and not for what I have to give."

THE LOVE LENS

When I was twenty-four, that rock-climbing helmet seemed outrageously expensive. Looking back, I see just how priceless Clayton's gift became in my life. It triggered a wondering in me. *Why do I believe love always has strings attached?* Each of us has our own unique experiences through which we translate life. No story is exactly alike, but there is one thing we all have in common: a broken love lens. We all need repair. No person is exempt because no person is perfect. I want to love Jesus more, and I know you do too, but our capacity to love will always be hindered by the condition of our love lens.

> NO STORY IS EXACTLY ALIKE, BUT THERE IS ONE THING WE ALL HAVE IN COMMON: A BROKEN LOVE LENS.

When you pour water onto a solid marble countertop, what happens? It spreads over the surface until it reaches the edge, and then it flows onto the floor. But what happens

> WE CAN'T BELIEVE IN GOD'S LOVE IF WE HAVEN'T FIRST RECEIVED IT. AND WE CAN'T LOVE HIM MORE IF WE'RE TOO BUSY TRYING TO FIX OUR LOVE LENS BY LOVING OURSELVES.

when you pour water onto a cleaning sponge? The porous surface soaks up the liquid. This is an illustration of God's love flowing into our hearts. He is always loving us, but we aren't always absorbing it. A heart with a broken love lens is like a marble surface. Any love Jesus pours on it falls to the floor. If we don't repair the damage, our ability to receive love will increasingly wane. But if we let him pull out the repair kit, our hearts can once again become porous to his affection.

Scripture says, "God is love. We love because he first loved us" (1 John 4:16,19). And as love, God "always protects, always trusts, always hopes, always perseveres" (1 Corinthians 13:7). We can't believe in God's love if we haven't first received it. And we can't love him more if we're too busy trying to fix our love lens by loving ourselves.

WASP NEST

Neil Anderson, a missionary and founder of Freedom in Christ Ministries, felt called to translate the Bible for the Folopa tribe in Papua New Guinea. He and his family moved to the rainforests of the southwest Pacific and engrossed themselves in the Folopa culture, learning their language and customs. Neil soon noticed that the tropical climate made plants grow a mile a minute. The Folopa cleared farmland only to have plants and weeds incessantly return and invade their crops. They cut down the plants, only to have new ones sprout soon after. The Folopa learned that "cutting down a tree does not kill it. Like weeds they keep coming back. Everything from above the ground may be dead and rotting, but the part that's left below is still alive. The following season, new shoots will be up, sprouting at one side or the other out of the trunk. A force below the ground has determined again to reach for the sky. That, they know, is where the life is. The top part, the part that shows, the part that one can point at and call tree, that's not where the life is. The life is at the base, in the bole, under the ground where you can't see. The Folopa know that if you haven't dealt with that, you haven't dealt with the real issue."[1]

When Clayton and I were dating, my heart was a hard surface. I didn't want to believe it, but Jesus used the rock-climbing helmet as an arrow to point to a place in my heart that needed healing. I was prone to doubt. Trust was excruciatingly painful. But God used Clayton's gentle loyalty to clean my love lens a bit. He also used my husband's love to reveal that I'd been trying to earn love from Jesus since I was eleven.

Your love lens may not be broken in the same area as mine, but I wonder, where *is* your love lens broken?

One time the Folopa had a problem with a swarm of

wasps living deep in the base of a tree. The wasps were dangerous to the young children in the village, causing their faces to swell. They became such a nuisance that the Folopa set out to destroy the nest with poison and fire, but it didn't faze the "one-inch, red-bellied menaces."

In the book, *In Search for the Source*, Neil describes how the entire tribe went to battle against the deadly wasps. When I read it, the description reminded me of a battle scene in a movie. Neil watched the Folopa prepare themselves for battle. Men danced around pounding their

> **LIKE AN ARTIST MOLDING A BLOCK OF CLAY, GOD DESIGNED US PERFECTLY.**

chests and stomping. They gave each other motivational speeches as they covered their skin with anything—cloth, leaves, branches—to keep the wasp needles from penetrating their sensitive skin. Then they moved in for the kill, attacking the tree with fire, burning the bark so that it would become weak enough to dig through to the roots. They burned and dug until they "split the stump open and exposed the nest." Unhappy wasps launched through the air and swarmed all around until a brave tribe member "reached in, grabbed the nest, and jerked it out. As he held it aloft there was a cheer of victory. But, though well-damaged, the tree trunk with the hole was still there. More wasps would come back. They continued their work of excavating the stump, finally pulling it out of the ground and rolling it down the long slope into oblivion. After that there was no more problem. They'd gotten the source."[2]

I wish I could give you a magic spell to fix your love lens, but it wouldn't work any better than insect spray did for the Folopa. Repairing our love lens isn't a walk in the park; it's a lifelong battle. If you want Jesus to soften your marble heart, you may have to do a courage dance and find someone to give you a pep talk as you put on your battle gear and start digging. When my love lens was broken with Clayton, his persistent pursuit of me was evidence of his sincerity. The fight to repair my love lens wasn't void of tension or hurt feelings, but Clayton insisted on weathering our storms together, rather than being torn apart by them.

God's love is persistent too, but sometimes we have a hard time seeing it. In Genesis, we read that God created us in his image. Like an artist molding a block of clay, God designed us perfectly. A perfect God fellowshipped with his perfect people (Adam and Eve) until they chose sin over him. Their decision planted a wasp nest in our hearts. The wasps in our souls are ruining our perspective, corrupting the way we interpret our creator's intentions. We've lost the ease of loving him more. But, thank the Lord, he's been on a mission to reunite us since our terrible divorce.

Since we can't believe in his love if we haven't first received it, let's look at three ways God has proven his love to us. I want us to finish this chapter knowing that

God's love toward us is great, and his faithfulness endures forever (Psalm 117:2).

3 PROOFS GOD LOVES US

1. THE FATHER CAME NEAR US

I can't get to know God over coffee. I can discover his character by reading my Bible, learning from my pastor, praying, and discussing him with friends. But these methods, however good they are, feel insufficient when I'm trying to get to know an intangible, all-knowing, all-powerful God on a personal level. Can you imagine how intimidating knowing God felt to people in the Old Testament?

The Hebrews didn't have a Bible, a pastor, the internet, commentaries, or Bible studies. The origin of their belief came from miraculous stories passed down by their ancestors: Abraham and Isaac, Jacob and Esau, Joseph, Moses, a cloud of smoke, a pillar of fire, manna from heaven, and the Ten Commandments. God understood that his people felt distant from him, so he came near. He instructed them to build the Tabernacle (a place of worship) and the Arc of the Covenant (a place for his presence). The Arc of the Covenant was a sacred box where God agreed to live among his people. The common person probably didn't feel intimacy with God through their tabernacle sacrifices or in the laws they followed, but they did understand the symbolism of the Arc. God, who created the universe, agreed to live in a box made by people so they could feel closer to him. By doing this, God was saying, "I will make my home among them; I will be their God, and they will be my people" (Ezekiel 37:27, NLT). Because he chose to come near, the Israelites felt loved and pursued by God.

But it gets better because God came even nearer.

2. JESUS ACCEPTED US

There was a 500-year gap in time between the Old and New Testaments. During this period in history, the Romans built an efficient road system, and the Greeks created a common language in and around the nation of Israel. These developments opened the door for a second love pursuit. The Jews thought God's next move would be to come as a mighty king, dominating, destroying, judging, and instituting justice on all their enemies. Instead, God came to us in the form of a tiny child from an insignificant village. A carpenter-turned-teacher, Jesus walked, laughed, ate, healed, wept, and served anyone and everyone but himself. He loved us in every way possible until the age of thirty-three, and then he loved us through the act of crucifixion.

"You see, at just the right time, when we were still powerless," Christ died for *us*. (Romans 5:6). It was the just-right time because people didn't believe that God loved them unconditionally. They obeyed strict laws, submitted to a police of priests, and sacrificed animals, hoping, but never *knowing*, if God was pleased. It was the just-right time because Jesus humbled himself to death on a cross so we could gain full access to his grace and finally be fully forgiven. It was the just-right time because the infrastructure lent itself to the rapid spread of Jesus' resurrection and power over death. "For God so loved the world that whoever believes in Him shall not perish but have eternal life. For God did not send His son into the world to condemn the world, but to save the world through Him" (John 3:16-17).

Jesus accepted us and restored our relationship with our Father. Are you starting to understand his humble pursuit? First, the God who made everything agreed to live in the Arc, and the creator became like his creation. Then he died and resurrected so we could live eternally. But his love pursuit didn't stop there.

3. THE HOLY SPIRIT HELPS US

Jesus knew that when he returned to heaven, Christ followers would feel abandoned, but his ascension unlocked a third love pursuit. Jesus explained why he had to leave like this: "it is for your good that I am going away. Unless I go away, the Advocate will not come to you; but if I go, I will send Him to you . . . But, when he, the Spirit of Truth, comes, he will guide you into all truth" (John 16:7, 13).

Jesus left so we could experience the third love pursuit—the Holy Spirit inside of us! Jesus didn't abandon us; he gifted us with the everyday presence of God. This is the closest fellowship God has had with humankind since he walked with Adam and Eve. The Holy Spirit shares every breath you breathe, every thought you think, every moment you live. The Holy Spirit is loving you as he does life with you: convicting, transforming, guiding, praying, and helping you. God the Father came near, Jesus accepted you, and now the Holy Spirit is helping you in any and every circumstance.

Appreciating God's love for us and his pursuit of us can take time. Currently, Clayton's favorite encouragement to me is, "Sharie, my number one goal in life is to make you happy." His actions prove his words true, but after eighteen years of marriage, I still have a hard believing how much he loves me. Why is my first impulse to make a mental list of all the times he's hurt me? Why do I want to doubt? If you've let God repair a broken love lens, but you're still struggling in a certain area, you may be fighting an internal battle between

> **JESUS LEFT SO WE COULD EXPERIENCE THE THIRD LOVE PURSUIT—THE HOLY SPIRIT INSIDE OF US!**

your sin self and redeemed self. I still doubt Clayton's love because there is a battle inside me between my sin self and my redeemed self.

The apostle Paul describes our battle inside like this: "I am unspiritual, sold as a slave to sin. I do not understand what I do. For what I want to do I do not do, but what I hate I do . . . For I have the desire to do what is good, but I cannot carry it out. For I do not do the good I want to do but the evil I do not want to do—this I keep on doing. Now if I do what I do not want to do, it is no longer I who do it, but it is sin living in me that does it" (Romans 7:15,19-20). We have corrupted love lenses because we have corrupted hearts. We were born into sin, but we were designed to be righteous. These two things create a battle inside us—between our identity before Christ, the sin self, and our identity afterward, the redeemed self. We can have a healthy love lens and struggle with loving God more than ourselves. I want to give you a practical picture of this battle so that you can recognize it in your own life and let go of any guilt you may have.

> **WE HAVE CORRUPTED LOVE LENSES BECAUSE WE HAVE CORRUPTED HEARTS.**

WORSHIP

I'm worshiping on the front row so that I don't get distracted. My hands are lifted and eyes closed. My mind and mouth are singing in unison. But then, without permission, my mind starts to wander. A little voice I call my sin self starts interrogating me during worship. "Is he really *everything* to you? Are you giving him everything? Really? *All* your heart? You're not! You're a hypocrite. How can you sing words that don't line up with your actions?"

Agony and confusion invade my mind. Should I lower my hands? Should I stop singing? Am I hypocrite?

A breath of sweet peace comes out of nowhere. My

redeemed self is fighting back. "Sharie, listen to me. Refocus. I hear the storm in your heart. Don't give up." I obey.

> Oh my God, my Father, my hope. There's
> no other. You're everything. Everything.
> You can have my heart. You can have my
> soul. You can have my life. You can have
> it all![3]

My mouth moves, but my soul is still worried that the sneaky sin self is trying to separate me from God's love again. I feel ashamed and alone. Who am I to sing words I can't live out? I don't belong in this service with these believers. I'm falling fast when my redeemed self comes to the rescue again. "Sharie, don't stop worshiping. Jesus is listening to the *part* of you who *wants* him to be your *everything*, to give him *all* your heart, soul, and life. Worship teaches your heart to believe what your soul knows. Keep pushing through."

> JESUS IS LISTENING TO THE PART OF YOU WHO WANTS HIM TO BE YOUR EVERYTHING, TO GIVE HIM ALL YOUR HEART, SOUL, AND LIFE.

THE SIN SELF AND REDEEMED SELF

Does this battle feel familiar? The apostle Paul described his soul raging like this:

I do not do the good I want to do, but the evil I do not want to do—this I keep on doing. So I find this law at work: Although I want to do good, evil is right there with me. For in my inner being I delight in God's law; but I see another law at work within me, waging war against the law of my mind and making me a prisoner of the law of sin at work within me. What a wretched man I am! Who will rescue me from this body that is subject to death? Thanks be to God, who delivers me through Jesus Christ our Lord! So then, I myself in my mind am a slave to God's law, but in my sinful nature a slave to the law of sin. (Romans 7:19-25)

You are not alone when you fail to love Jesus more. Paul wanted to do good, but he often gave into evil. Why is the battle between your sin self and redeemed self so torturous? Because you were originally made in God's image. Your identity was attached to him. Your love for him was connected to your love for yourself. We weren't designed to have to choose between loving him or ourselves. But Adam and Eve separated us from our original identity when they sinned. Your redeemed self is fighting to restore your original nature while the sin self is trying to keep you in slavery. Just like the Folopa persevered in their battle against the wasps, we too must be determined in our battle between our sin self and our redeemed self. Fighting sin isn't easy, but our freedom is worth the battle.

I read a true story about a boy in Vietnam who trained his monkey to do his bidding. The boy's neighbor watched the boy and his monkey and decided this was his opportunity. You see, the older man loved tea, but the tea leaves he preferred were in a hard-to-reach area on top of a mountain. So the man obtained his own monkey and fed it opium water every night. After the monkey developed an addiction to the substance, the man took it to the top of the mountain and taught it which leaves to harvest. Soon, the monkey spent every day harvesting leaves. Soon, this slave monkey produced a significant profit for the boy's neighbor.[4]

> YOUR REDEEMED SELF IS FIGHTING TO RESTORE YOUR ORIGINAL NATURE WHILE THE SIN SELF IS TRYING TO KEEP YOU IN SLAVERY.

God didn't design this monkey with a natural craving to opium. But when the man introduced opium into the poor creature's system, the monkey became a slave to the substance and to the man as a result. You weren't created with an addiction to sin, but the fall in Eden now causes it to flow through our veins. Ever since you were born, you've developed a familiarity with the sin self. But when you came to know Jesus, "you were set free from sin and have become [a slave] of God, the benefit you reap leads to holiness, and the result is eternal life. For the wages of sin is death, but the gift of God is eternal life in Christ Jesus our Lord" (Romans 6:22-23).

You and I are no longer slaves to sin, but we will still experience its familiar pull. The apostle Paul felt this pull as well, and he learned this secret: If we want to be free from sin, we must make ourselves slaves to God—we have to chain ourselves to him. We can wean ourselves from our sin addiction by becoming dependent on the Holy Spirit instead. Let's end this chapter by talking about how the Holy Spirit empowers our redeemed self.

> **IF WE WANT TO BE FREE FROM SIN, WE MUST MAKE OURSELVES SLAVES TO GOD—WE HAVE TO CHAIN OURSELVES TO HIM.**

SUPERHERO OR HOLY SPIRIT?

I'm driving my son home from pre-school in our super-cool minivan. While my mind is occupied by thoughts of how the salesman talked me into purchasing an automobile shaped like an oversized Dustbuster, my five-year-old son sits in the back seat wondering about the Holy Spirit. He interrupts my moping with a theological question. "Mama, how does the Holy Spirit *get in you?*"

"Well, Jacob, when you ask Jesus to be your Savior and

the ruler of your life, he sends the Holy Spirit to live in your heart."

"Yeah Mom! I *know that!* I want to know *how. How* does he get in your heart?"

Seriously, kid. Are you sure you're five? "Well, Jacob. Do you remember John Paul on *Super Friends?* He's the green guy who can fly through anything? Well, the Holy Spirit is a lot like a superhero. He flies through your skin and gets into your body. Does that make sense?"

"Yeah, Mom. Thanks."

This explanation would probably not hold up in a theological debate, but it helped my Jacob connect with the Holy Spirit a little bit more, and that was enough for this minivan-driving mom. I didn't even know the Holy Spirit was on my young son's radar, but I was thankful to know that Jacob was curious about this Spirit living inside him.

Have you ever become overwhelmed and *amazed* that the Holy Spirit lives inside you? When God's Spirit lived inside the Arc of the Covenant, the Israelites had to handle the sacred vessel properly. The Arc was never to be touched because the Spirit inside was so powerful. One time, a man named Uzziah died trying to stabilize it, and another seventy people died trying to peek inside it (2 Samuel 6, 1 Samuel 6:19). When God commanded the Israelites to carry it around Jericho, the walls crumbled to the ground. And when the priests carried it through the river Jordan, the waters parted (Joshua 6:4, Joshua 3:15).

The same Spirit that lived in the Arc of the Covenant, parted the waters, and brought down Jericho's walls lives inside every believer. But our sinful, mortal bodies could not house the Holy Spirit if Jesus hadn't covered our sin in his blood. His blood protects the believer and opens the door for the Holy Spirit to do life with us. The Holy Spirit is our most powerful helper, coach, and guide, but we forget him all the time. We're so busy trying to prove we are "more than conquerors" that we forget that the power to overcome comes from him and not ourselves. We're so busy *trying to love Jesus more* that we forget that the Holy Spirit is in us to help us. If Paul were teaching us, he would say,

> **WE'RE SO BUSY TRYING TO LOVE JESUS MORE THAT WE FORGET THAT THE HOLY SPIRIT IS IN US TO HELP US.**

> If Christ is in you, then even though your body is subject to death because of sin, the Spirit gives life because of righteousness. And if the Spirit of him who raised Christ Jesus from the dead is living in you, he who raised Christ from the dead will also give life to your mortal bodies because of his Spirit who lives in you . . . we are more than conquerors through him who loved us. For I am convinced that neither death or life, neither angels

nor demons, neither present or future, nor any powers neither height nor depth, nor anything else in all creation, will be able to separate us from the love that is in Christ Jesus our Lord. (Romans 8:10-11, 37-39)

Don't let your sin self make you feel distant from God. God has been on a mission to bring you closer to him your entire life. God's complexity and bigness can be intimidating, but they don't have to keep you from intimacy. Instead of trying so hard to prove that you love Jesus more, stop and take a breath. Rest in the conquering power of Jesus' love and tune your mind into the powerful guidance of the Holy Spirit. You are a conqueror in Christ. You "don't belong to those who shrink back and are destroyed, but to those who have faith and are saved" (Hebrews 10:39).

> **YOU ARE A CONQUEROR IN CHRIST.**

CHAPTER 2

I Love You More with My Past

"It's so much easier to fix things on the outside than the inside. The inside is just so complicated."
—Joseph King (my son when he was ten)

MY PAST

Dinner is over, so we move into the living room to continue our trip down Memory Lane. We're just a group of friends telling secrets, stories, and funny quips. They have me rolling in belly-busting laughter until my friend from the past says, "Sharie, I'm glad we've gotten to know each other as adults. When we were kids, I thought you were spoiled and stuck up."

The words fly through the air like arrows, stabbing me in the heart. I sit still and breathless. I don't know how to respond, so I laugh it off. But I can feel the tears coming, so I excuse myself. "Well, I'm tired. Let's call it a night."

I put my face in my pillow, hoping it will absorb my hurt feelings and tears. What did I do to earn such a scathing childhood review? Little-girl Sharie felt anything but arrogant. She felt afraid and alone. She wanted to live anyone's life but her own. My husband is right beside me, but I don't have the energy to share, so I choose to hide my emotions in my dreams.

I rise early to escape the wretched discomfort. The car is loaded, and as we wave goodbye, a floodgate of pain flows from my eyes. Because my husband is amazing, he tenderly asks what's wrong. So I start my story.

When I was in elementary school, I spent the first moments of every day in my stepfather's clutches. He brought me into his bedroom to satisfy his perversion while my mom got ready for work in the hall bathroom. When it was time for me to get ready for school, my stepdad carefully made it seem like we were simply cuddling before my mom came to get me.

The trip to the bathroom was excruciating. I wanted to take a long, hot shower to get rid of my filth and shame, but that would make us late. So I covered myself with school clothes instead. I stared in the mirror as mom brushed my hair. I could see that my eyes reflected the pain in my soul, but my mom was preoccupied. She was concerned about all things school: Are you ready? How are your friends? Are you doing well? Is your lunch packed? I didn't want to answer her superficial questions, so when my brother woke up, I welcomed a distraction.

School offered a predictable and safe environment. I could forget that girl in my mom's bedroom and become someone new for the bus driver, my friends, and teachers so that no one would discover my secrets. I was determined to hide behind my blue eyes and pigtails. If I hated who I was in that room, surely they would too. I'd give them the better version of me: good student, Field Day athlete, baton-twirling-parade girl, and soccer star. That was the best side of me. That was the side they wanted to see. Perhaps hiding my pain made me seem stuck up?

I lived a double life on and off for about five years. When I turned ten years old, home life became difficult for my mom too. Fights at home became more frequent, so Mom became more consistent with our church attendance. Church made me feel safe, loved, and happy. I remember sitting at a wooden desk, staring at a picture of Jesus on the wall, and thinking, "He seems so loving." And then while sitting cross-legged on the shag carpet in my Sunday school room, I heard the story of God rescuing the Israelites from slavery, and it moved me to tears. I longed to be rescued too, but I was afraid to ask for help, especially from my mom. I had to keep her love intact because she was everything. I couldn't risk telling her. What if my confession caused her to hate me?

I had to free myself. I determined I would no longer let my stepfather take me from my room. The next morning, he came and shook me, but I didn't budge. He shook me again, but I refused to rouse myself. I lay stiff, face planted in my pillow, screaming in my mind for him to leave. And in this very fearful moment, I prayed my first prayer to a God I didn't yet know.

> **"GOD, IF YOU SAVED THE ISRAELITES, COULD YOU PLEASE SAVE ME?"**

"God, if you saved the Israelites, could you please save me?" Sweaty and scared, I waited. When I couldn't feel my stepfather's presence any longer, I peeked from my pillow in time to see him turn toward my door and walk away. When he came again the next morning, I mirrored what I'd done the previous morning, and he left and never came back.

Sometime later, my mom picked me up from day care in tears. On our drive home, she divulged that my stepfather was seeing another woman. A confusing swirl of emotions gurgled in my heart, rising and rising, until an explosion erupted from my mouth. Extremely out of character, I screamed at the top of my lungs, "Well, I hate him anyway! I don't know why you didn't leave him a long time ago!" In a second, my mom's concern for herself shifted to me. She pulled into the driveway, entered our house, sat next to me, and ministered to me.

That very day, a terrified Sharie revealed as much as she could to a mother she loved dearly and never intended to betray. I feared she would see me as "the other woman" too. We hugged and cried for what seemed like hours. Soon after, my mother and stepfather divorced, and we moved in with my grandparents. Living with my Nanny and Granddaddy, I came to understand Father God as my rescuer and Jesus as my Savior.

IGNORANCE ISN'T BLISS

A lot of you have a story like mine. Some of you have experienced greater pain, and others less. No story is exactly the same, and even if you haven't experienced abuse, you've experienced some sort

> **YOUR PAIN IS VALID BECAUSE IT IS A PART OF YOUR HEART. BUT JESUS IS GREATER THAN OUR PAIN.**

of heartache. Whether it's the death of a friend or family member, a disease, or a mistake from the past you can't shake, pain is universal. Your pain is valid because it is a part of your heart. But Jesus is greater than our pain. If we're willing to love Jesus more with our past, I know he can bring peace to situations that have tormented us. For five years, I shoved my abuse into a dark place in my heart. I was afraid to bring it into the light because I felt disgraced. I thought hiding my secret would bring greater relief than seeking help. But being tough doesn't get you through; it makes you bitter.

There are a few coping mechanisms our bodies use against pain. When people suffer or experience trauma, their minds will often block out the experience in order to move forward. I've also seen people begin to remember their lives differently, creating a false reality. These methods may temporarily soothe our pain, but in the end, ignorance isn't bliss. Ignorance doesn't change our past, and it can't heal our hearts. Ignorance is a prison that will hold you back from a hope-filled future.

Something released in my soul the day I told my mom my story. The heavy weight I'd been carrying lifted, and I no longer felt alone. Proverbs 17:22 says, "A joyful heart is good medicine, but a crushed spirit dries up the bones." Hidden pain crushes the human heart, but God says, "I know the plans I have for you . . . plans to give you hope and a future" (Jeremiah 29:11). If we learn to love Jesus more than our past, he will help us stop living according to what we see in the mirror and start living for who we want to be.

REMOVING SPLINTERS

A friend knocked on my door slightly panicked. "My son got a splinter on the playground. Do you have tweezers?" We walked to the bathroom, and I pulled out my splinter-removal kit. It contained pointed, rounded, square, and tilted tweezers, cotton balls, hydrogen peroxide, a safety pin, straight pen, toenail clippers, antibacterial cream, and bandages. When I placed the entire assortment on the countertop, her eyes widened. "You're prepared," she said.

I grinned and explained, "Splinters are Jacob's number-one nemesis. Every removal method I've tried yields the same results: anxiety, shaking, crying, and panicking. Sometimes he starts screaming before I've even touched the wound. I've decided his anxiety is more rooted in his anticipated fear than the actual removal

> **HE LOVES YOU MORE THAN YOU LOVE YOURSELF.**

of the splinter. He wants me to get the splinter out, but he fights against me the entire time. One time, I removed the splinter and tried to show it to him, but he was too busy screaming to notice. So I gently tapped his shoulder, and when he saw the sliver between the tweezers, he replied, 'I didn't even feel that.'"

When you ask Jesus to heal you, the process may be difficult, but Jesus will be gentle. He loves you more than you love yourself. He loves you more than *anyone*. Jesus once told his closest friends, "In this world, you will have trouble. But take heart! I have overcome the world!" (John 16:33) Jesus has overcome the world. This includes your pain. He wants to teach you to overcome it too. Your sin self is trying to convince you that ignorance is bliss. It is trying to convince you that the pain of healing isn't worth the victory. But your redeemed self knows that Jesus can heal your hurt completely. It will take courage to bring the shadows of your past to light and take the steps you need to heal.

My healing has felt like peeling an onion. The hurting place is deep inside, but Jesus doesn't hand me a knife and tell me to slice out the center. Instead, he places the onion in front of me and instructs, "Let's peel these back one at a time. Each layer will reveal some pain, but I will heal as you peel. I'll tell you when I think you're ready, and you can choose how deep we go."

I want to help you love Jesus more with your past, but this chapter is not an all-inclusive manual on emotional healing. It is meant to be a seed of faith to help you believe that Jesus can bring peace to a hurting or regretful soul. The first step out of ignorance and toward healing is to set our minds free by thinking outside the box.

OUTSIDE THE BOX

Jesus is tired from teaching a crowd when evening comes. He and the disciples load themselves in a boat to travel to the Gentile side of the Sea of Galilee. Exhausted, Jesus decides to nap in the front while the disciples row until a violent storm rages on the sea. Even though many of these men had been career fishermen, the sea intimidates them. Fearing for their lives, they wake Jesus, who rises and stills the waves and winds with his voice. The silent sea causes the disciples to wonder, "Who is this? Even the wind and the waves obey him" (Mark 4:41). They don't know that an even greater miracle is coming.

Their journey ends on the shore of a place called the Gerasenes. A man full of demons meets Jesus on the shore. The people used to bind this man with chains, but his demon strength tore through the chains. Now he is a wanderer. He spends his days in the remote hill country and the tombs crying out and cutting himself with stones. He is in a prison of pain. Everyone is afraid of him. He hurts himself, and I'm sure he hurts others, but God didn't create him to be this man. "When he saw Jesus from a distance, he ran and fell on his knees in front of him. He shouted at the top of his voice, 'What do you want with me, Jesus, Son of the Most High God? In God's name don't torture me'"(Mark 5:6-7).

Jesus sees beneath his foreboding exterior. When he looks at the man, Jesus sees a hurting child—his father's creation—and he knows that whatever past circumstances led to his condition can be overcome in that moment. Jesus casts the demons out of the man and into a flock of pigs. The man becomes well, but the demon-possessed pigs dive into the sea destroying themselves. The villagers are furious because these pigs represented many of their financial investments. Motivated by their loss, they demand that Jesus and the disciples leave.

Let's pause for a moment.

In the middle of this storm between Jesus, the demons, and the townspeople is a man who has been delivered and is now in his right mind. He turns toward the townspeople who've been afraid of him for years and then glances at Jesus and the disciples. Where does this delivered man belong? He begs Jesus to take him into the boat, but "Jesus did not let him, but said, 'Go home to your own people and tell them how much the Lord has done for you, and how he has had mercy on you'" (Mark 5:19).

Why does Jesus say no? It seems like it would serve them both well for Jesus to take the man from the Gerasenes along. He could be the poster-child disciple. "Come see the disciple Jesus delivered from demons, and be healed yourself!" What a great campaign slogan. But Jesus was thinking outside the box. His main focus was this man's health. While it seemed inhumane for him to leave the man in the world of his past, Jesus wanted to teach him to run *to* the pain and not *from* it. Jesus wanted the man to return home as a victor and not a victim.

BELIEVE YOU ARE A VICTOR, NOT A VICTIM

When I came to know Jesus, there was a moment of utter satisfaction, but then my thoughts shifted. *If Jesus saved me, why do I have to stay on earth? Why can't I leave this tiresome world?* I wondered. I can imagine the delivered man, kneeling on the shore after his healing. Perhaps he rises to watch Jesus, and the disciples row away. And then he stands by the Sea of Galilee, waving until he can no longer get a glimpse of the boat. Finally, reality sets in. He remembers all the things he's said and done to the people back home. He wonders how many children he's terrified, possibly even his own. He wonders if anyone will trust his healing enough to give him a place to call home. Will anyone love or hug him again? I can feel his shame and doubt. With Jesus gone, the man has two choices. He can become a victim again, returning to what he's always known—a lonely life wandering among the tombs and hills. Or he can return home and fulfill Jesus' calling as a victor.

I wonder how long it took for the man to prove he was trustworthy. Did people question whether his healing was permanent? Would he remain in his right mind, or would the demons return? I was sitting in an audience when Lysa Terkeurst said, "You can't be a victim and a victor at the same time." The demon-possessed man chose to be a victor on the shore that day, but I'm sure there were many challenging days when he had to make the difficult choice all over again. If I had been this delivered man, I would have had to remind myself of Jesus' visit every day. I would have had to believe that he crossed the sea just to save me. Think about it. Jesus traveled with the disciples through a storm, pulled up to the Gerasenes, delivered this man, and then got back in the boat and rowed away. Jesus didn't take the man with him because he wanted the man to live out his healing in front of the people who had seen him sick.

I never thought I had anything in common with the demon-possessed man. I'm not a man. I've never been possessed. I've never been chained down or broken said chains with my demon strength. I have never lived in a graveyard. The demon-possessed man and I are so very different, and yet we are also similar. We've both felt lonely and isolated in our suffering. We've both longed to belong but couldn't because we had something to hide. We've both wanted to be free but felt trapped. We were both pursued by Jesus and healed. And we were both challenged to use our story to glorify Jesus.

We have to make a choice between victor or victim. The man from the Gerasenes had a long road to walk toward his healing, but he chose victory. Scripture gives us a few glimpses of his faith. In Mark 5, the passage where Jesus told him to go home, it also says, "So, the man went away and began to tell the people of Decapolis how much Jesus had done for him. And all the people were amazed" (Mark 5:20). Obedience initiates God's action. The man returned home and did what Jesus asked, and the people were amazed.

> **WE HAVE TO MAKE A CHOICE BETWEEN VICTOR OR VICTIM.**

In Mark 6, Jesus and the disciples return to the man's town, and this happens:

> As soon as they got out of the boat, people recognized Jesus. They ran throughout that whole region and carried the sick on mats to wherever they heard he was. And wherever he went—into villages, towns or countryside—they placed the

sick in the marketplaces. They begged
him to touch even the edge of his cloak,
and all who touched it were healed.
(Mark 6:54-56)

The man Jesus delivered in the tombs changed an entire village, but he couldn't have done this if he kept himself in the past. When you feel yourself sliding into victim
mentality, choose to be a victor instead.

The devil wants to keep us captive to our pain. In the
midst of our pain, we may wonder, *Where is Jesus, and why
doesn't he take my problems away?* Remember, Jesus healed the
demon-possessed man, but he didn't take the man out of
his situation. If we think outside the box, we see that the
tough challenge of returning home was part of the man's
road toward victory instead of a punishment. Jesus left
heaven to heal us and is
now in heaven praying
for us to live in victory.
We are not alone be-
cause nothing can sepa-
rate us from his love (Romans 8:35-39).

> WE ARE NOT ALONE BECAUSE
> NOTHING CAN SEPARATE US
> FROM HIS LOVE.

PUSH THROUGH

I'm riding a bus through the streets of India. There are
no lanes, just incoming and outgoing vehicles honking,

cows plopped in the road, motorcycles, rickshaws pulled by men riding bikes, street vendors, children running, and dogs scavenging. The air smells of trash fires, curry, diesel, animals, and tobacco. India is alive. Crowds of people live in close proximity to each other. Our bus finds a dirt road, which deposits a layer of dust on my face. As we pull up to the orphanage, I remove the grit with a fresh wipe. Everyone exits the bus except for one girl. We're gathered in a cluster outside the bus when we hear her scream. I pop up the bus stairs in time to spy a sly monkey steal her banana. The long-tailed burglar escapes leaving my friend flustered, but unharmed.

Giggles flow from our eyes. We don't want to stop telling and re-telling what just occurred, but the kids are waiting, so we shift our attention to the adoption-home parents. After a few hours of fun and games, our bus guide leads us home. Little do we know, he has a prank planned. Instead of taking the normal route, he drives us through an animal preservation area. He stops on the side of the road and motions us to exit. "Come, come," he says and hands us each a pomegranate, instructing us to peel them. A dozen monkeys appear out of nowhere, stealing the fruit from our hands. They crouch nearby, peeling, picking, and putting the pomegranate seeds in their cheeks.

I learn something from these monkeys. They know what they want, and they're not afraid to push through to get it. Are we so different? Scrolling through my social media feed, I find a selfie taken at a conference a while back—I'm running through a corridor with a massive group of ladies behind me. I dramatize my panic in the picture as a joke, but I do remember thinking, *Are these ladies going to trample me?* I'm surrounded by women who all want to get the best seat in the house. They want to be close to

> **WHAT ARE YOU WILLING TO PUSH THROUGH TO LOVE JESUS MORE WITH YOUR PAST?**

Beth Moore. And, really, so do I. It's my first time attending Living Proof, so I join in the frenzy. Perhaps we hoped if we got close enough, some of her godly mojo would rub off on us.

What are you willing to push through to love Jesus more with your past? Do you have a passion to be whole, or are you content where you are? How do you want your past to influence your future?

We were dating when I asked Clayton, "Do you wish you could change parts of your past?"

He confidently replied, "No. My experiences made me who I am today."

No one had ever given me that answer. Everyone always had at least one thing they wanted to change. My shameful past made me assume he was lying. I dreamed of splicing out entire sections of my life so I could be "normal." But we can't edit our souls like a film. We either heal, or we hurt.

Sometimes it's hard to recognize hurt. It disguises itself. It's not always red and raw. It doesn't always look like sobs and sadness. Hurt can make us indifferent and intro-spective, unemotional and unexcitable. Unable to hope or dream. Unwilling to love or be loved. It will steal who we are and rob us of who we want to be.

Clayton and I were sitting under moonlight on metal bleachers when I confessed the abuse of my past. I thor-oughly expected him to toss me aside like a used rag. I was so sure he'd refuse me because I wasn't pastor's-wife material. But he didn't. Instead, he looked at me and said, "Sharie, knowing who you are today and where you've come from makes you even more beautiful in my eyes."

I had *hoped* Clayton would see my healing heart, but I honestly expected the opposite. I've finally come to a place where I've made peace with my past. I'm not trying to slice and dice away the parts chaining

> JUST BECAUSE LIFE IS FULL OF TROUBLE, PAIN DOESN'T HAVE TO BE OUR CONSTANT COMPANION.

me down. Just because life is full of trouble, pain doesn't have to be our constant companion. I've learned that my husband was right. My regrets haven't disappeared, but pushing through them has shown me that they have made me who I am today.

So I need to ask again. Do you have a passion to be whole, or are you content where you are? How do you want your past to influence your future? I want to intro-duce you to a woman who pushed through for her healing.

THE BRAVE WOMAN

Jesus is on an important mission for an important man. He's on his way to heal a man's twelve-year-old daughter when a brave woman enters the scene. The brave woman is pushing her way through the crowd because she's been bleeding for twelve years. Doctors have tried to help her, but she keeps getting worse. Societal rules dictate that she should not be in this crowd, much less touch a holy man. But she's tired of feeling plagued, ostracized, and unlovable. She needs relief, and she will push through to get it. So she does. The brave woman isn't going to stop the busy teacher because she doesn't want to draw attention to herself, so she simply grazes the end of his robe with her hand. The tiny touch sends power flowing through her body. The sides of her mouth smile as she pauses to soak in the moment. But then, the teacher speaks. "Who touched me? Someone touched me; I know that power has gone from me" (Luke 8:45-46). She tries to sneak away, but his eyes pierce hers. "Seeing that she could not go unnoticed, [the woman] came trembling and fell at his feet. In the presence of all the people, she told why she had touched him and how she had been instantly healed. Then he said to her, 'Daughter, your faith has healed you. Go in peace" (Luke 8:47-48).

There are two pieces of advice we can learn from the brave woman.

1. WHEN YOU FEEL LOST IN THE CROWD, BELIEVE THAT JESUS SEES YOU

This woman had worn her shame for so long, she didn't even ask for Jesus' healing. She was afraid to bother, to touch, or to stand out. When we feel insignificant, Jesus notices us. Jesus asked who touched him and wasn't willing to leave for his next healing appointment until she spoke up. Why did he ask her to speak up? Because he wanted her to know he'd seen her. He wanted to declare her healing in front of everyone. He wanted to announce that she was healed and set free. He didn't want her to hang her head any longer!

2. WHEN THE PAIN OF YOUR PAST RETURNS, REST IN HIS PEACE

Although Jesus heals us, we will not fully forget our past. When those feelings surface, read Psalm 17:8 "Keep me as the apple of your eye; hide me in the shadow of your wings." Jesus sees you, healed

> YOUR IDENTITY IS NOT ROOTED IN THE SITUATION HAUNTING YOU, BUT IN YOUR SAVIOR WHO HEALS YOU.

you, and protects you. Don't fall back into a victim mentality, but rest in his peace. Your identity is not rooted in the situation haunting you, but in your Savior who heals you.

People inevitably questioned this woman's healing,

but when they did, I bet she remembered Jesus' words, "Daughter your faith has healed you. Go in peace and be freed from your suffering" (Mark 5:34). When people doubt your healing, you don't have to explain yourself. Focus your faith where you want to grow. When you focus on your fear it gets bigger, but when you focus on Jesus, fear takes a back seat.

MY PRESENT

When I was in college, I wasn't sure marriage could work for me. I knew God created it, but I'd been through so many marriages and divorces growing up that I didn't want to give it a try. I loved Jesus, but I honestly thought the single life was preferable. But then I returned home from a mission trip to find that the construction on my college apartments hadn't been finished yet. I ended up living with my campus pastor's family. I watched them work—husband and wife, father, mother, and children. God used their family to plant a seed of hope in my heart; this could be my future.

I look at the treasure of a family God has given me today. Our life isn't perfect, but my husband and I have fought to heal, grow, and protect our marriage. Sometimes we stare at the stars together and wonder at the miracle Jesus has worked in our lives. My husband was almost aborted, but his mother decided to give him an incredible life with Joe and Jane King instead. My home life consisted of multiple relationships joining together and pulling apart. But today, Clayton and I have loved each other faithfully for eighteen years, and we have two amazing boys. This wouldn't have been possible without our Savior's grace and a lot of perseverance.

Hebrews says, "Therefore, since we are surrounded by such a great cloud of witnesses, let us throw off everything that hinders and the sin that so easily entangles. And let us run with perseverance the race marked out for us, fixing our eyes on Jesus the pioneer and perfecter of our faith" (Hebrews 12:1-2a). In Jesus' day, if a follower needed to focus on their calling or a commitment they made to the Lord, they would take a Nazirite vow. Beth Moore describes this vow:

> Those who took the Nazirite vow were to allow their hair to grow long as a physical sign of special devotion to God. That way, if they temporarily forgot their vow, the quickest glance in a mirror would remind them. Also, others would ask why they let their hair grow so long, and this would give them an opportunity to testify about their devotion to God.[5]

I don't know where you are on your journey of healing—if it's progressing, or if you feel like you keep stalling. But I am confident Jesus can do a miracle in your life if you choose to love him more with your past. Maybe you simply need a reminder to choose to think outside the box, believe you're a victor, and push through your pain to find your freedom.

> YOU SIMPLY NEED A REMINDER TO CHOOSE TO THINK OUTSIDE THE BOX, BELIEVE YOU'RE A VICTOR, AND PUSH THROUGH YOUR PAIN TO FIND YOUR FREEDOM.

What kind of physical sign could you display to remind you of your spiritual journey toward healing? If you can't think of one yourself, perhaps you could phone a friend for ideas and accountability. Please know I am praying for you to see yourself as the apple of our Savior's eye so that you too will "throw off everything that hinders and the sin that so easily entangles and run with perseverance the race marked out for *you*, fixing *your* eyes on Jesus the pioneer and perfecter of *your* faith.

CHAPTER 3

I Love You More Than My Perfection

> *"To love righteousness is to make it grow;*
> *not to avenge it."*
> — Philip Yancey, *Disappointment with God*

CHALKBOARD ON THE WALL

I'm trying to make spaghetti while my two young boys are conducting testosterone tests on one another, and I'm about to lose it. My husband and I have discovered that the boys usually morph into monsters the third night he's away, so I'm just trying to survive until he pulls in the driveway. I'm pouring the noodles in the water when disaster strikes. To this day, I'm not sure what happened or how it happened, but Joseph is lying on the ground screaming, and Jacob is defending himself profusely. There's no way I'm going to get an accurate account of the situation because it's "he said, he said." I send them to their rooms and walk back into the kitchen to dish out dinner and place it on the table.

"Dinner's ready. You can come out." But only one teary face appears. I figure Jacob is cooling down, so Joseph and I sit and eat together.

I'm carrying dishes to the sink when I feel a tender tap on my arm, "Mama. I think you need to come to Jacob's room." Together, we creep to Jacob's door and listen. Inside I hear him pacing and punishing himself, "I never do *anything* right. I'm *always* messing up. I just don't belong in this family!" His repetitive and forceful self-accusation breaks my heart, so I tenderly open the door and ask for permission to enter. As I pass his chalkboard wall, I notice he's covered his behavior chart with big red X's and frowny faces. He's in a pit, and I need to help him out.

He calms himself and confesses, "Mama, I'm always hurting Joseph. I don't mean to, but I can't help it. I just don't think I can be a good Christian. I think God is mad at me, and I don't belong in this family."

I sit and stare at him lovingly. Whatever I say has got to be good because this kid is a natural-born lawyer—weak reasoning won't work. Jesus gave me the words I needed.

"Jacob, you are part of this family. When you mess up, we will fix the problem together. You're not alone, and we would never abandon or trade you in. If Joseph had messed up like you, do you think I would put him in the car, drive him down the road, and leave him to fend for himself because I've had enough? No way. You are my boys, and we're in this together. I love you for who you are, not how you behave."We hug a lot, and when he is ready, go get his dinner. Walking out, I notice something new on Jacob's chalkboard wall. While we were talking, Joseph sneaked in and wrote, "Jacob does belong in this family. He's the best brother EVER!"

GOD IS IN LOVE WITH YOU, NOT PERFECT BEHAVIOR

I wish I could say I was as good of a sibling as Joseph is to Jacob. When *my* brother and I were younger, we got along pretty well, but when I turned twelve, I could no longer tolerate how obnoxious, hyper, *all-boy* he was. One unfortunate night, we got into a pretty heated fight, and he wouldn't obey me (go figure). I lost my temper, took my two palms, and pushed his chest, hoping he'd plop to the floor . . . but we were standing at the top of a flight of five stairs. He toppled down and then landed in between the bottom stairs and the open bathroom door.

I had *never* pushed him like that before, and I loved him, so I was about to run down the stairs to hold him and tell him I was sorry when my mom's voice sounded behind my head. "Sharie! What have you done? Tell your brother you're sorry! *Now*!" Her command brought a monster out of me. I really have no idea where my next statement came from because I never talked back to my mom in this manner, but I said, "No! If I apologize, then I'll be sinning *twice*. Once by pushing him down the stairs, and again by saying I'm sorry when I'm really not."

Ironically, I was sorry. And I was going to tell him I was sorry before she asked me to. I was being rebellious for sure. Mom sent me to my room and gave me a spanking. I can probably count the number of spankings I received on two hands, so I wasn't skilled at getting them. After my mom swung once, I turned over, and my knee caught her second swing, spraining her wrist. She always told me that a spanking hurt her more than it did me, but this was the first time I believed her. My mom drove a standard-shift Volkswagen Rabbit, so every time she had to shift with her sprained wrist, she cringed, and I regretted my rebellion all over again. I soon offered to shift for her. She'd push in the clutch, and I'd shift the gears.

When we were created in God's image, God didn't design us to sin. So when we fall, it's natural to wonder, *What's wrong with me?*

Adam and Eve were the first ones to experience the shift from complete perfection to sin's infection. I used to perceive the story of Adam and Eve as the beginning of the end of a wonderland. I used to believe God loved his children every day . . . until they messed up. Then, he kicked them out of the garden and commanded an angel with a fiery sword to keep them from all things good. A few years ago, though, the Lord challenged me to look for his grace, instead of judgment, in the Old Testament. Rereading Genesis 3, I learned that God is in love with *us*, not our perfect behavior.

ADAM AND EVE

The serpent approaches Eve and asks, "Did God really say, 'You must not eat from any tree in the garden?'" (Genesis 3:1). The woman says to the serpent, "We may eat fruit from the trees in the garden, but God did say, 'You must not eat fruit from the tree that is in the middle of the garden, and you must not touch it, or you will die.'" (Genesis 3:2). The serpent is trying to plant seeds of doubt in Eve's heart. He continues, "You will not certainly die. For God knows that when you eat of it, your eyes will be opened, and you will be like God knowing good and evil" (Genesis 3:4-5). The woman's trust wavers.

> GOD IS IN LOVE WITH US, NOT OUR PERFECT BEHAVIOR.

Why would God keep something from her? She was designed in God's image. She wants to know God fully as she is fully known by him. Why would God allow the serpent to know something she doesn't? The serpent isn't telling the woman an outright lie. God *is* keeping knowledge from Adam and Eve. He is protecting them by giving them all things good and keeping them from all things evil. The serpent tricks the woman into feeling betrayed by her creator. He tricks her into trusting herself more than God. She doesn't know that her lack of knowledge is a precious gift, so she listens to the serpent, trusts herself, and eats from the forbidden tree. The man eats too, and they become different. Afraid of this difference, they hide.

The Lord knows they are different because our Lord knows everything. They disobeyed him, and sin has now entered their souls. Still, God doesn't come with hot fists, yanking Adam and Eve from the bush, brandishing his fiery vengeance. He walks toward their hiding spot "in the cool of the day" (Genesis 3:8) and calls out, "Where are you?" (Genesis 3:9) Adam answers from the bush, "I heard you in the garden, and I was afraid because I was naked; so, I hid . . ." (Genesis 3:10). The Lord knows the answer, but asks anyway, "Who told you that you were naked? Have you eaten from the tree I commanded you not to eat from?" (Genesis 3:11) The man and woman don't know what to do with their sin, so Adam blames Eve, and Eve blames the serpent (who is pleased with himself). After they are finished pointing fingers, their father explains the consequences of their bad decision. And after he is finished disciplining, the Lord ministers to his children, replacing their fig leaves of shame with clothing that will last. Then the father does something that used to break my heart. He banishes them from the garden and places cherubim with a fiery red sword to guard the tree of life.

Why does God keep Adam and Eve from life? Because

sin has now become a part of their identity. God doesn't want them to eat from the tree of life, living forever with the curse of their sin. They were designed to live forever, so the Lord gives them the gift of dying so that after Jesus' resurrection, they can be restored to their original design and fellowship with him eternally. Adam and Eve messed up, but God doesn't give up. Instead, he puts into motion a plan of redemption and reconciliation.

PERFECTION ISN'T WHAT WE DO, BUT WHO WE BECOME

Here's the truth. The minute Adam and Eve sinned, God would have been justified to snap his fingers and destroy the human race with a single thought. He didn't. He could have given them lifetime community service hours to earn back access to Eden, but God knew sin could not be overcome by human work. So our loving Lord pursued his children (Genesis 3:8), was patient with them (Genesis 3:9-13), defended them against the serpent (Genesis 3:14-15), disciplined them (Genesis 3:16-19), covered their shame (Genesis 3:21), and developed a plan of restoration (Genesis 3:22-24). God chose grace over judgment. He came up with a plan to bring us back to him. He doesn't expect perfection from us; he works it in us. If this is God's plan, why are we working for our perfection instead of receiving his purification?

I remember walking down the sidewalk, one child in each hand, toward their preschool classes. I was embarrassed because they looked absolutely absurd. Joseph was wearing Spiderman pants, a face mask, and a Batman cape, and Jacob had insisted on wearing his new reversible basketball uniform even though it was winter. I forced him to at least wear sweatpants and a long-sleeved shirt underneath. He looked like the Michelin® guy, but I was tired of arguing. I was signing them into their respective classes when Jacob's kind teacher walked over and whispered, "We know when they dress themselves, so don't worry." I breathed a loud sigh and walked away feeling oh-so-much-better! But as I drove myself home, I couldn't explain to myself why I was carrying such ridiculous mom-shame. Was I worried people would judge my children by their clothing style? Or maybe it was a deeper issue. Perhaps I worried people would think I couldn't control my kids' behavior. This was the deep-rooted issue. I was so very worried about people's perceptions because I wanted people to think I was a good mom.

As my parenting progressed, I realized that mothering isn't about controlling behavior; it's about shepherding the heart. Parenting isn't about teaching our kids to be faultless; it's about walking with them as Jesus transforms their little (and not-so-little) hearts.

This teacher's words set me free. Instead of arguing about clothes after that, I let my kids wear whatever they liked. Sure, I got some stares, but I had fun with it and forgot to care somewhere along the way. This is the kind of freedom I hope you can find. "Bring what you have, no matter what it looks like. His standards are embarrassingly low, and

> SALVATION ISN'T ABOUT DOING BETTER; IT'S ABOUT LETTING JESUS TRANSFORM YOU INTO SOMEONE NEW.

he will work with what you're willing to put in his hands. You are imperfect, but you can be perfectly used by him."[6] Salvation isn't about doing better; it's about letting Jesus transform you into someone new. Paul explains this in Philippians: "Therefore, my dear friends . . . continue to work out your salvation with fear and trembling for it is God who works in you to will and to act according to his good purpose" (Philippians 2:12-13).

Salvation is a process. We were saved the day we met Jesus, but as we continue to live on this earth (battling with our sin self), we continue to work out our salvation. This process is called sanctification. Sanctification is the journey of discovering how to live like Christ in a world that isn't governed by his principles and in a body that doesn't always want to love him. Sanctification is hard work, so very often we cheat by trying to do what he "expects" instead of becoming who he created us to be. When we focus on what we're doing instead of who we're becoming, we put the cart before the horse. God wants to teach us how to *be* before he teaches us what to *do*, or at least he wants us to learn *how* to be *as we are doing*. Who we are becoming is more important than what we are doing, but who we are becoming should be evidenced by what we are doing. If we think Jesus loves our perfect behavior, we become obsessed with performance. But if we understand that our identity is rooted in his love, we can focus on becoming. I've noticed three ways we tend to pursue perfection in Christ. Two are influenced by doing, and one is influenced by being: fighting *for* perfection, fighting *against* perfection, and fighting *from* perfection.

WHAT FIGHTING FOR PERFECTION LOOKS LIKE

I was walking beside our Israeli tour guide, listening and learning. We came to a light just as three Orthodox Jewish men crossed the road. They kept their heads bowed, eyes staring at the street as they walked toward us. Suddenly, one of them ran into a pole, hitting his head and almost falling in the middle of the road. He managed to catch his balance without looking up, and as he neared us, he drew his shoulders

> WHO WE ARE BECOMING IS MORE IMPORTANT THAN WHAT WE ARE DOING, BUT WHO WE ARE BECOMING SHOULD BE EVIDENCED BY WHAT WE ARE DOING.

together squeezing his arms into his belly. Without a word or a glance, the three men plowed through our group. I could tell they were annoyed by our presence. Our guide explained, "They are very legalistic in their customs. They would rather hit their heads and pass out in the street than look at and lust after a Gentile woman."

Their legalism may seem ridiculous, but in Orthodox Jewish circles, their standards are admirable. These men are probably considered the picture of perfection among their peers. Similarly, I worked very hard in college to be a good Christian. I served on our campus ministry team and took mission trips every summer. One semester, our campus pastor organized 7:00 a.m. prayer meetings every Tuesday. I had perfect attendance until I woke late one morning. I'd stayed up until 2:00 a.m. working on a project and slept through my alarm. I was frantically trying to pull myself together when my dear roommate said, "Sharie, God will still love you if you skip prayer. He won't punish you for being human."

> **FIGHTING FOR PERFECTION IS MOTIVATED BY FEAR.**

"I know, but they are expecting me," I said as I stumbled out the dorm room.

Waiting and staring at the elevator door, my redeemed self convicted me. I came to the realization that I had sincerely believed God would love me more if I made myself into the person he expected me to be. I let go, released a gigantic exhale, turned toward my room, and plopped back in bed.

Fighting for perfection is motivated by fear. We're afraid that Jesus won't love us, we will fail, become corrupted, or never overcome our sinful nature. Legalism seems like an easy solution because it's thrilling to feel like we've fought for perfection and won! Overcoming our sin feels satisfying. "Look what I did, Jesus! Aren't you proud of me?" But if our identity is rooted in our works, what happens when we fail?

One night I walked toward my dorm feeling condemned. I couldn't think of a specific sin I needed to confess—I was just feeling inadequate. Frustrated, I called my campus pastor for advice. He said, "Sharie, look your sin in the face, and instead of defending yourself, confess your wretchedness. Then, claim your freedom through Jesus' blood, not from yourself!"

His advice hurt my pride. Did he think I was wretched? What had I done to earn that bad opinion? I wanted to defend myself because I hadn't "done" anything wrong. I was so very worried that my good behavior hadn't been noticed by my campus pastor or the

> WHEN WE TRY TO SAVE OURSELVES, WE BECOME EASY TARGETS.

Lord. And then my redeemed self said, "Sharie, you need to follow his advice. You're trying to be perfect on your own, but Jesus is the source of your perfection."

Here's the truth. When we try to save ourselves, we become easy targets. All Satan has to do is make you feel like a failure, and boom!—you're condemned. Jesus "has saved us and called us to a holy life—not because of anything we have done, but because of his own purpose and grace" (2 Timothy 1:9a). You are called to a holy life because Jesus chose you, not because you're super spiritual. "Brokenness isn't something to hide but to integrate into our lives . . . without our imperfections, there is nothing to place in the hands of God."[7]

If you want to love Jesus more than your perfection, you have to place your legalism in his hands. Let Jesus reveal your motives. Are you afraid? Are you trying to prove something to Jesus, to others, to yourself? We can't love Jesus more than our perfection if we're trying to earn it ourselves.

WHAT FIGHTING AGAINST PERFECTION LOOKS LIKE

When I became a Christian, I learned that the church expected your best. Wear your best clothing, put on your best face, and be on your best behavior. Sitting stiff in my church pew, quiet as a mouse, I gawked at all the perfect people surrounding me. I hoped to be like them one day—they were pictures of excellence. But as I got older, I noticed imperfections seeping through people's whitewashed walls. Two teenage friends sneaking kisses in the church bathroom. Hushed conversations about the youth pastor's quick exit. Gossip, judging, fighting, and families falling apart were all in the church while my Christian school friends started using drugs and partying. Christians didn't seem so perfect anymore.

The church (and our world) has become disenchanted with perfect people. Communication streams are buzzing: *No One is Perfect, No Perfect People Allowed, You Were Born to Be Real, Not Perfect, Sorry, I'm Not Perfect . . . but I'm Not Fake Either*, and *You Be You*. When I first heard these messages, they seemed to bring freedom, like a breath of fresh air. But recently, these same phrases seem to be shifting—from intending freedom to justification. I've noticed two Christian camps forming—the law-leaners who fight for perfection, and the grace-givers who fight against it. Grace-givers can't stand the pesky little law-leaners. They shake their fist at traditional Christianity, screaming, "No one is perfect! We need to love sinners." But in the grace-giver's passion to be against perfection, they've forgotten their calling to be perfect. We are called to be gracious and loving, but we are also called to be holy. 1 Peter 1:15 says, "Just as he who called you is holy, so be holy in all you do; for it is written: 'Be holy, because I am holy.'" Matthew 5:48 says, "Be perfect, therefore, as your Heavenly Father is perfect." The overactive grace-giver skips past these verses because they gravitate toward a kinder, nicer, more inclusive grace—a grace that doesn't require conviction, change, or growth. But what the overactive grace-giver doesn't understand is that he or she is changing the nature of grace by separating it from the law. One of my favorite authors, Lisa Whittle, describes this division in her book, *Put Your Warrior Boots On*:

> We've made grace too easy. It has become a crutch and thereby cheapened the costly price of it, which, for our Savior, came through sacrifice and death . . . Yes, grace is beautiful, but it came through holy and righteous grit. It came through torture and abuse and injustice and thorns and mockery and fear and hatred and flimsy believers chanting right along with the secular folks. Grace came through the commitment and conviction of the Father and the cruelty of the cross, and without that first, there would be no beautiful home of grace for us to live in now. So, let us understand that our conviction to live a life of grace depends on our level of commitment to the cross. Not on our empty Christian buzzwords. Not on our taking the easy way out by believing our behavior really doesn't matter. Grace isn't just another excuse to live without consequence. Jesus didn't die for that.[8]

The church is not made up of two tribes—law-leaners who fight for our perfection and grace-givers who fight against it. We are *one* tribe, *one* church, *one* people, *one* body of Christ. When we remove either law or grace from the process of perfection,

> **WE ARE ONE TRIBE, ONE CHURCH, ONE PEOPLE, ONE BODY OF CHRIST.**

we cannot properly pursue perfection. But when we marry the two, we purify ourselves by fighting from the perfection Jesus has already given. Christ did not die so that we could take advantage of his grace. He died to *give* us the advantage of his grace.

WHAT FIGHTING FROM PERFECTION LOOKS LIKE

We were traveling to Disney World by plane. My boys were young. It wasn't their first flight, but they were starting to notice everything. Before we took off, the luggage was being loaded, and you could hear grinding beneath the plane. Joseph asked, "Daddy, what's that noise?" Because Clayton had morphed into vacation mode, he didn't offer the technical illustration, but a colorful one. "Well, Big Joe. This plane runs on Tom-and-Jerry power. There's a wheel under the plane. When Tom and Jerry start running, the plane takes off, and when they stop, we land." The entire flight, Joseph kept hoping Tom or Jerry didn't get too tired. He knew we needed them both for the plane to work. In the same way, a cartoon with just Tom or just Jerry wouldn't fly because they go together. (Pun intended.)

I know that is a super silly story and completely unspiritual, but similarly, working out our salvation requires the law *and* grace. The two attributes work in balance—work isn't greater than grace, and vice versa. Rather, the two work in communion. If we are fighting from the perfection Jesus has already earned, we can love both the law-leaner *and* the grace-giver. Jesus pursued the Jew *and* the Gentile. He shielded the woman caught in adultery (John 8:1-11) and had dinner with Simon, the Pharisee (Luke 7:36). He delivered a Gentile man from a legion of demons (Mark 5:1-20) and converted a Jew who killed Christians named Saul (Acts 9:1-19). He forgave Peter for his denial (Mark 14:66-72) and the criminal on the cross for his lawlessness (Luke 23:43).

Jesus didn't come to eradicate the law, but to complete it (Matthew 5:17). By itself, the law enslaved people, so Jesus married the law to grace because neither does its job alone. When we fight from perfection we accept the jobs of law and grace in our sanctification: conviction and forgiveness, perseverance and blessing, love and discipline, pain and healing. We need the law to reveal the gravity of our sin, and we need Jesus' grace to cover and save us from it. Jesus uses the law and grace in harmony; they function hand in hand to make us holy as he is holy.

Now that we've talked a little about how hard it is to love Jesus more than our perfection, I want to address our need to love others who are trying to do the same. Whenever we learn about God, we learn not only who we're supposed to become, but also who we are supposed to become for the world around us. So, let's talk about how to create a safe place for our friends to work out their salvation. I call this the judgment-free zone.

GRIPING AND GROCERIES

The automatic doors slid as I walked through and grabbed a metal cart. I leisurely sanitized the front of the cart and proceeded through the grocery store, aisle by aisle. I strolled, collecting my food, analyzing the ingredients, and placing them carefully in my cart—heavy things on the bottom and breakables on top. When my list was completed, I pulled up to the only open checkout line behind the mom with the screaming kids. I stared as she shoved candy down her children's throats like a mother bird feeding her hatchlings and wondered why she would give fussy kids candy. She must have sensed my judgment because she gave me a perturbed look. I glanced at the tabloids but couldn't stop assessing the situation, *If she'd cut back their sugar intake, they'd be much more controllable. When I have kids, they'll never scream in public!*

Fast forward a few years. The doors open automatically. He wouldn't eat in the car, but I've driven all this way. Maybe Jacob can hold out for a three-item stop: baby gas drops, diaper wipes, and a nursing bra. Two items down, now I just need the nursing bra. Trying on bras is pure misery, but I need one, so I squeeze the stroller into the changing room. My mission is almost complete when a small whimper escapes Jacob's car-seat canopy. When I peek through the slit, his whimper turns into a full-volume wail. Shirtless with sweat running down my back already, my stress level shoots sky high. I should get him out to feed him, but I'm not thinking clearly.

"Jacob, this will only take a minute, baby. Give me a minute, and we're outta here!" Cry. Wail. Scream. "I guess that's a no." *Why am I talking to an infant?* In the middle of my crisis, the lady in the next stall offers me third-person unsolicited advice.

"Mommy, I'm hungry. Feed me." I pause. *This lady is instructing me in the voice of a child from the next stall?* Then she does it again! "Mommy, I'm hungry, feed me." I am a stressed-out and postpartum mess, so I slump on the stall seat, cry, and defend myself to myself. *I just needed three things. I can't do this mother thing.* I dress myself, unpack my basket, and head to my minivan, empty-handed.

Fast forward a few more years. The doors open automatically, and as I grab a green cart with one hand, I use my other hand and my entire bodyweight to sling Joseph's infant seat safely inside the cart. *Where did Jacob go?* Of course, he's in the fresh foods section picking and piling grapes into his mouth! Griping and groceries has begun. The next thirty minutes sound like this: "Come here, Jacob. Walk beside the cart. Stop taking things off the shelf and putting them in the cart. I have an idea! Can you keep one hand on the cart *at all times*? Come on, baby . . . the cart isn't supposed to drag you. Your job is to walk . . . "

I finally pull up to the checkout line, thinking I'm home-free, when I see Jacob to my right. He is worshiping the rows of perfectly-placed candy. He lunges toward the packages of goodness, grabbing and slinging them everywhere. Exasperation is in the air. Do I smile and load food on the conveyor, or deal with the candy mess?

"You don't need that candy, son. Can you put it back on the shelf for me?" The sneaky look in his eyes tells me he's thinking, *This goodness is EXACTLY what I need!* He grabs a package. I take it away, and in my peripheral vision notice the girl trying to look away. She reminds me of myself once upon a time. One cart. Perfectly loaded. Probably questioning my parenting abilities and making judgments. Looking at that young girl who is looking away from me, I realize I'm living out each undeserved and disparaging judgment I sent another poor mother's way. I am convicted.

THE JUDGMENT-FREE ZONE

I had a lot of strong opinions about parenting until I had a child. I assumed people with depression simply needed to pray, sing, and read their Bible until I struggled with postpartum depression. It was intimidating to read "be joyful always" when I was looking up to see the ground. Only then did I regret my misinformed opinion. Here's the bottom line: We are a bunch of imperfect

> **JESUS WANTS TO GIVE US SPACE TO FAIL AND GRACE TO GROW.**

people trying to let God perfect us inside a messed-up world. Wouldn't it be easier to fulfill our calling in a judgment-free zone? Jesus wants to give us space to fail and grace to grow, so he commands, "Do not judge, or you too will be judged, for in the same way you judge others, you too will be judged, and with the same measure you use, it will be measured to you" (Matthew 7:1-2).

If we don't want to be judged, why do we judge? Here are some reasons I have judged:

- I knew better, so I could "help" them change.
- I had already learned that lesson, and I wanted to save them the trouble.
- I saw their "true" intention or motivation and needed to call them out.
- I was tired of how someone's behavior affected me.
- I wanted to "open" their eyes to the truth.
- I wanted what they had.

Well, that felt shameful! Judging is ugly. We judge when we feel morally or spiritually superior. Judging flows from pride. A judgment-free zone is only created when we fix our eyes on Jesus instead of each other. Each person's transformation process looks different. Only the Holy Spirit can convict or change a person's heart. Just like we want Jesus to teach us, we need to trust him to teach the people around us what they need to learn and when and how they need to learn it.

> **EACH PERSON'S TRANSFORMATION PROCESS LOOKS DIFFERENT.**

But what if they don't *want* to learn it? Here's the truth: If others refuse to receive conviction from God, they certainly aren't going to listen to us.

How do we trust God with our unresponsive friends? I like Mary DeMuth's advice, "You can pray. You can love. You can sacrifice. You can obey God. But other than that, you cannot convict someone of sin. And when you try, you assume God's position in your loved one's life. You shortchange the Almighty's plan."[9] Perhaps Jesus is waiting for that just-right moment when our friend is ready to change. If we step in to fix our friend, we might get in the way of his process. When we create a judge-free zone, we open the door for God's conviction in our brother and sisters' lives.

Do you remember when Jesus and the disciples were invited to eat with Mary and Martha? I imagine Mary and Martha were probably both busy preparing before Jesus started teaching. But maybe Mary (who reminds me of my sneaky, but super-sweet Joseph) couldn't stay focused on dinner when Jesus was dishing out heavenly food in the next room. Mary starts listening by the doorway, peeling a potato. And before you know it, she is skipping out on all the cook-

> WHEN WE CREATE A JUDGMENT-FREE ZONE, WE OPEN THE DOOR FOR GOD'S CONVICTION IN OUR BROTHER AND SISTERS' LIVES.

ing duties. Martha might have known this would happen. Perhaps Mary is more of a people person, and Martha has always taken up the slack. Perhaps this time Martha wanted to be the one soaking up Jesus' goodness, but she can't let go of her duties.

Martha is mad, so she slings her judgment through the air, hoping Jesus will discipline Mary as well. "Lord, don't you care that my sister has left me to do all the work by myself? Tell her to help me!" (Luke 10:40). In other words, Lord, why does she get to skip out on the dinner preparations? She is lazy. She is irresponsible. I want to be in there too, but I'm the responsible one. Can you make her responsible too? Jesus diffuses the situation, making it a judgment-free zone: "Martha, Martha, you are worried and upset about many things, but few things are needed— or indeed only one. Mary has chosen what is better, and it will not be taken away from her" (Luke 10:41-42). Martha thought she knew what Mary needed, but she didn't. Her judgment sat on deaf ears. Jesus wanted Mary to enjoy his presence while she could, and he invited Martha into the room as well by saying, "you are worried about many things, but few are needed." Perhaps he was communicating, "We don't need a big meal. Come and sit too."

What happens when you shake a soda can violently and then pop the top? Oxygen mixes with the carbonation, and then soda fizzes violently out of the opening onto your hand and spews out everywhere. When we're focused on doing, behaving, and fighting for our perfection, we can become internally aggravated at people who supposedly aren't carrying their own weight. We want them to earn God's favor too. We think that an explosion of judgment will give us the satisfaction we're looking for, so we let our insides erupt and feel better . . . for a quick minute. Like a soda can, we experience momentary release, but deep down, we're still resentful.

However, if we're willing to tune in to Jesus' voice, he will bring us back down to earth, asking, "Why do you look at the speck of sawdust in your brother's eye and pay no attention to the

> MAYBE GOD WILL USE YOUR LIFE OR WORDS TO CONVICT A FRIEND, BUT YOUR CONVICTION SHOULD NEVER COME IN THE FORM OF JUDGMENT.

plank in your own eye?" (Matthew 7:3) Maybe God will use your life or words to convict a friend, but your conviction should never come in the form of judgment. Judgment is not our calling.

Loving Jesus more than our perfection is hard work, but it is possible. I want to leave you with two things as we end this chapter. If you're having a very imperfect day, remember this quote from Bob Goff: "Our successes often distract us, while our failures usually shape us."[10] And then, remember I'm praying this over your life: *I thank God for the work he is doing in you through this book, and I pray for you with joy because I'm "confident of this, that he who began and good work in you will carry it out on to completion until the day of Christ Jesus"* (Philippians 1:6, emphasis mine).

CHAPTER 4

I Love You More Than My Position

"I find we are always at our best when we are serving."
— Caroline Barnett, *Willing to Walk on Water: Step Out in Faith and Let God Work Miracles Through Your Life*

PLEATHER SEATS ON A SCHOOL BUS

I don't enjoy waiting for the school bus. It's either freezing, raining, or impossibly hot. I don't want to be here. I liked shopping for the new clothes and school supplies. But now, all day, every day, I'm told where to sit, how to walk, and to do my homework. I can't wait until I grow up and people stop telling me what to do. Presently, I'm sitting in my desk waiting for that school bell to announce my freedom.

I don't enjoy the bus ride home either. The blazing pleather seats on this yellow school bus make the back of my thighs sweat buckets. If only I could fall asleep . . . but the wheels keep going round and round, bouncing and banging my head against the glass window. A man in a luxury car races past, angry-faced, honking and shaking his fist. The bus driver yells at the rebels behind me. They've dissected their cassette tapes and are flying the insides like a kite. Unfortunately, the plastic disk on the end is scraping every car that passes. Maybe if they hadn't been so rude, I could've asked that luxury-car man for a ride on his perfect-temperature plush seats. I can't wait until I own car. For now, I'm thankful my bus stop is next.

As I hike down my driveway, the birds chirp, celebrating my afternoon of freedom. I open the door to a different kind of chirp.

"Why don't you play outside and get some fresh air before dinner?" My grandmother's request sounds like a question, but I know it's not. *Groan.* Our backyard is a child's paradise, but my pouting makes it a prison. I sit on a railroad tie and sulk. When I think I've soaked up enough vitamin D to please my grandmother, I tiptoe inside toward the television.

"Is that you, Sharie? Wash your hands and set the table. It's time for dinner." Dinner is followed by my homework, a shower, brushing my teeth, and bedtime. So much for freedom! I can't wait until I'm in charge of myself.

GROWING UP IS A POSTURE, NOT A POSITION

Did your little-girl brain trick you into believing that growing up was about reaching a magical age where no one
had power over you? First, I thought it was sixteen. *When
I get that car, I can go anywhere!* But then I discovered that
gas costs money. Then college represented the epitome of
individualism . . . until I was tied down by a syllabus full
of boring books and forty-page papers. Surely a job with
a paycheck was the answer! But then, rent, insurance,
and groceries ate my pay-
check before I could enjoy
it. It took me awhile, but
I finally realized that re-
sponsibilities always increase, and commands never cease.
Growing up isn't a place you reach; it's who you become.
It's a posture, not a position.

> GROWING UP ISN'T A PLACE YOU REACH; IT'S WHO YOU BECOME.

When my son, Jacob, was little, he assumed that my
brother was older than I was because he was taller. He
thought that height determined age. So I asked him,
"Have you noticed that Uncle Chase is taller than Nanny? Who do you think is older—your great-grandmother
or your uncle?" This was certainly confusing. He looked
at her grey hair and soon understood that height doesn't
determine age. Just like height doesn't determine age, neither does position determine prominence.

We can't love God more than our position if we're trying to measure it by what we see. Growth by position looks at the outward appearance, but postural growth is determined by the inside demeanor. All I have to do is look in the mirror to see new wrinkles or grey hair.

> JUST LIKE HEIGHT DOESN'T DETERMINE AGE, NEITHER DOES POSITION DETERMINE PROMINENCE.

A face in a mirror is easy to examine, but a soul is much less tangible. Just as a person's height doesn't determine their age, neither does their age determine their growth. Just because someone *is* grown up doesn't mean *they've* grown up. Maturity isn't proven by position, but posture.

America has taught us that we have the right to life, liberty, and the pursuit of happiness. I'm writing this chapter because I'm afraid we're pursuing happiness at the expense of our lives, at the expense of our freedom, and certainly, at the expense of our souls. Have we abused our souls in order to make happiness our slave? We all have a choice. We can keep letting the pursuit of our success, goals, and dreams run our lives, or we can learn how to love God more in our position so that we can find rest. If you're ready to learn, let's look at King David's life.

THE SHEPHERD

Jesse is worried about his other sons on the battlefield, so he sends David to deliver food and bring back word of their condition. David is the newly anointed king, but he's currently bi-vocational—shepherding for his father and serving King Saul as an armor-bearer and soul-soother. I'm sure he wonders if being king is only a dream. David arrives and runs straight to his brothers on the front line. The armies are shouting the war cry when a giant of a man, Goliath, starts spouting threats toward the Israelite army. David asks for an update. Goliath has challenged the Israelites for forty days, but no one will go out and face him. Soon, David's questions have earned him an audience before King Saul. David says to Saul, "Let no one lose heart on account of this Philistine; your servant will go and fight him" (1 Samuel 17:32).

Looking down at David, Saul assesses the boy in front of him. Insignificant shepherd. Musician. Good-looking and possibly a brave armor-bearer, but this boy is certainly no victor. Saul rejects David's offer. "You are not able to go out against this Philistine and fight him; you are only a young man, and he has been a warrior from his youth" (1 Samuel 17:33). Looking up at Saul, David digs deep to explain his soul's motivation. I am a shepherd. When I protected my sheep from the paw of a bear and the paw of a lion, the Lord protected me. Why would the Lord not do the same when I shepherd his nation? Saul concedes, "Go, and the LORD be with you" (1 Samuel 17:37). But there's doubt in his mind, so he offers David his armor. David humors the king by trying it on, but Saul's enormous armor swallows David alive. "'I cannot go in these,' he said to Saul, 'because I am not used to them.' So he took . . . his staff in his hand, chose five smooth stones from the stream, put them in the pouch of his shepherd's bag and, with his sling in his hand, approached the Philistine" (1 Samuel 17:39-40).

You know that David killed Goliath with a single stone from his sling, but the people in the moment did not. What do you think was running through Saul's mind as David marched toward the Philistine army? Perhaps he thought, "Kid, couldn't you have worn my armor? You're making me look bad." If you were a soldier or one of David's brothers, would you have been cheering him on, or accusing him? "If rocks could kill Goliath, we would've done that forty days ago." And finally, when Saul's armor didn't fit, why didn't David ask for someone else's? Surely *someone* was close to David's size!

David didn't search for suitable armor for the same reason he didn't acquire a sword, develop a military strategy, or wrangle some soldiers as a

> **DAVID DIDN'T EXPECT THE WIN TO COME FROM HIM.**

backup plan. David didn't expect the win to come from him. David was with the sheep when God called him to be king, and he kept that posture when God called him to confront Goliath.

When God chose Saul to be Israel's first king, Saul was "small in his own eyes" (1 Samuel 15:17). He obeyed the Lord and accepted the prophet, Samuel's, advice. As Israel grew in prominence, Saul lost his lowliness. He didn't want the win to come from God. He wanted it for himself. So he became a king no longer used by God, but rather one who was trying to *use* God. He thought that

> **POSITIONS OF POWER HAVE THE PROPENSITY TO ROB US OF OUR PROPER POSTURE.**

stealing God's kingdom for himself would bring satisfaction, but it robbed his peace instead. He no longer felt protected, and fear became the driving force behind his decisions. His obsession with power caused him to lose his mind (he was literally tormented by demons), his children, his kingdom, and his life.

Here's the truth: Positions of power have the propensity to rob us of our proper posture. The broken part of us, our sin self, longs to feel significant, and dare I say, prominent. We want to be noticed, appreciated, and loved by people. But we weren't created to receive glory, but to give glory to our Savior. If we want to love Jesus more than our position, we have to take the proper posture.

King Saul and Goliath the mighty warrior may have judged David as a foolish boy. But who looked more foolish after David slung his sling and stood before Saul holding Goliath's head? Goliath sure looked intimidating puffing out his chest as he mocked the Israelites, but how feeble he appeared falling from a single stone to his head. Saul seemed like a splendid king until he cowered behind the faith of a shepherd boy because he was unwilling to face Goliath himself. David took off Saul's armor and ignored Goliath's jeers because he knew that God would use his shepherd's heart to defend himself.

Maybe this teaching feels completely irrelevant because you don't feel influential. I disagree. In 2 Corinthians 5:20, Paul says you are God's ambassador to the world. You are a daughter of the King of the universe. God will use you to help others know him and to disciple those who already believe. You influence your friends, family, kids you babysit, co-workers, employees or employers, sports teams, social media bubble, and your small group or Bible study. So when you're given the privilege to lead, you get to choose whether you will put your confidence in your position or your posture.

HOMESCHOOLING

It's one of those Sunday mornings where I'm trying to leave, but I've run inside fifteen times. Why is the diaper bag empty? Why did you take off your shoes? Where's your sippy cup? Etc.

We're running late, but I'm feeling a little relieved to be on the road when an argument breaks out between my seven-year-old and me. I'm not giving him his predicted answer, so he's presenting his case from a variety of perspectives. He's good, but I'm putting up an adequate defense. After an exhale of exasperation, I realize, "I am arguing with a seven-year-old who is not going to stop. Why am I doing this to myself?" As we pull into the church parking lot, I announce, "I refuse to argue! Get ready for church." My boys and me walk into church mad and frustrated.

I drop them off in the kid's area, thinking to myself, "Sharie, you just have to keep it together two more weeks before their teachers get to deal with them all day!" This is my first year of freedom. Both of my boys will be in elementary school! I can't wait.

I'm late for the worship service, but I haven't missed all the singing. I close my eyes to let go of my morning and think to myself, "This is the year the Lord gives me my life back." But the Lord responds, "Sharie, there are character traits Jacob needs to learn, which his teachers won't have time to teach. Will you homeschool him?"

Pouty face. Crying. I can't sing now, Lord! The rest of the day I feel like throwing up, but I pull up my laptop and search, "homeschool curriculum." Scared to death, I say yes.

If you fast forward four years, I'm still homeschooling. But my boys are bigger, and therefore, more manageable. I've created a little space in my life for speaking and writing when I hear the Lord speak again, "Sharie, you need to make yourself small. If you make yourself small, I will do big things." Confession: My response was aggravation. "I've been putting my dreams on the shelf for years for the sake of my husband, our ministry, my children . . . you name it, Jesus. Don't you think it's my time to reap a little?"

> **I NEEDED TO LET JESUS INCREASE, AND I NEEDED TO DECREASE.**

Despite my resentment, my gut is telling me that "making myself small" is the next step in my Jesus journey. This is certainly not the "calling" I felt like I deserved. But soon, I realize it's the greatest calling I've ever had. Somehow, someway, I needed to let Jesus increase, and I needed to decrease (John 3:30).

STAYING SMALL MAKES YOU STRONG

People always ask me, "What's the hardest thing about being a woman in ministry?" My answer to this question is not just for women in ministry, but for every woman. Women are driven to make a difference, but we have to juggle a lot to make it happen. Our dreams don't always pay, and doing them alone feels impossible. We naturally spend energy on our husbands and children, and then we feel guilty when we take some for ourselves. We look for someone to coach, invest, train, and support us, but when (and if) we find someone, the investment feels greedy. Our path is untested, and paving a new one feels insurmountable. So we put our dreams back on the shelf.

Do these struggles resonate with you?

When Jesus called me to make myself small, I was

afraid. If I become less in this world full of people fighting for themselves, who will take care of little ol' me? I already feel so very small. How do I let myself become less in a world where it's so easy to be overlooked, forgotten, mistreated, unnoticed, or abandoned?

If we want to love Jesus more than our position, we have to make ourselves small. This may create fear in your heart, but take comfort in this: if Jesus can love you more than his life, he can teach you how to love him more than your life.

Philippians 2:5-9a in *The Message Bible* says this:

> Think of yourselves the way Christ Jesus thought of himself. He had equal status with God but didn't think so much of himself that he had to cling to the advantages of that status no matter what. Not at all. When the time came, he set aside the privileges of deity and took on the status of a slave, became human. Having become human, he stayed human. It was an incredibly humbling process. He didn't claim special privileges. Instead, he lived a selfless, obedient life and then died a selfless, obedient death, a crucifixion. Because of that obedience, God lifted him high and honored him far beyond anyone or anything, ever.

Jesus was God, but he didn't consider equality with God as something he could use to his advantage. Jesus *made* himself human, considered his life *nothing*, and *gave* himself over to death for three days. What did his obedience earn? Father God exalted him to the highest place!

When God asked me to make myself small, my sin self was afraid to lose everything. If I make myself nothing, what will I have left? Nothing?

No! Not nothing. When we make ourselves nothing, we inherit everything because no one can take from a person who has nothing to lose. Jesus traded his home in heaven for a humble human birth in a cave of animals. When he left home to minister, he traveled from one city to the next, not knowing where he'd spend the next night. When Jesus loved sinners, the

> HE MADE HIS LIFE WORTH NOTHING SO HIS FATHER COULD GIFT IT BACK TO HIM. HE KEPT NOTHING TO GIVE US EVERYTHING.

Jews disowned him. When he tried to tell people he was God, the Romans declared him an enemy. When Jesus submitted his life to crucifixion, all the disciples except for John abandoned him. Hanging on the cross, Jesus could have chosen to claim his rightful position as King instead of loving us more, but he knew something I hope to learn. *Equality with God was not something to be used to his own advantage.* His father asked Jesus to sacrifice his position, so Jesus obeyed. He made his life worth nothing so his Father could gift it back to him. He kept nothing to give us everything.

There is someone who craved equality with God. When Satan was an angel, he said in his heart, "I will raise my throne above the stars of God; I will sit enthroned on the mount of assembly, on the utmost heights of Mount Zaphon. I will ascend above the tops of the clouds; I will make myself like the Most High" (Isaiah 14:13-14). He challenged God to a battle of King of the Mountain. But since he was not greater, he lost and was thrust from heaven to face a destiny of eternal damnation (Revelation 12:7-17). Then God created man and woman in his own image. This enraged the sneaky serpent, so he tempted Adam and Eve with the same desire to be like God. Mankind gave in, and ever since, we've struggled with loving ourselves more than we love Jesus. We are insecure in our sin, trying to make it better by making ourselves bigger. But this is certainly a battle we will lose.

> **THIS IS THE SECRET TO LOVING GOD MORE THAN OUR POSITION: TO MAKE OURSELVES NOTHING AND LET HIM DO THE LIFTING.**

When we love our position more than God, we're trying to win King of the Mountain against an all-powerful God. Hiking up the mountain, our redeemed self knows we should bow, but our sin self tricks us into battling God instead. We want our blessing like Jacob. The mountaintop view tempts us to take what we deserve instead of letting go of our kingdom in order to become a part of his. Taking up our cross is a hard message to live. We can't do it unless we're willing to emulate Jesus who gave up equality with God for our sake. When Jesus gave up everything, God exalted him to the highest place. This is the secret to loving God more than our position: to make ourselves nothing and let him do the lifting.

Has your calling become bigger than the One who called you? Well, it's your lucky day! I've got two more secret weapons to help you love God more than your position.

MOTHER TERESA

As Mother Teresa walked the streets of Calcutta, she became burdened to open a hospital for people who were left to die in the streets. One day, just as a reporter arrived to observe the sisters, a man from the lowest caste arrived in an ambulance. Mother Teresa brought the injured man inside and asked two nuns to care for him. One of them was a girl from a high caste named Sadhana. It was her first day, and since she'd come from privilege, the reporter doubted Sadhana's ability to care for the dying man. "Dirt covered his body so thickly it had to be scraped off. Some sores teamed with maggots. Other sores stunk so badly of gangrene that even the maggots had died."[11] But Mother Teresa knew Sadhana needed to discover if she could live out the calling she'd chosen. Accompanied by a more experienced nun, Sadhana scraped and cleaned the man's skin with a forced smile. When she could no longer hold her stomach, she suddenly excused herself. The reporter patted himself on the back, but three hours later, Sadhana sprinted toward him and Mother Teresa shouting, "'I cleaned him!' The reporter, astonished, asked, 'What made it possible? What did Mother Teresa say to you?' Sadhana said, 'Mother Teresa told me to do it for Jesus. I have been touching the body of Christ for the last three hours.'"[12]

SELF-CONTROL IS THE KEY TO SATISFACTION

I didn't tell this story to make you feel guilty, but to get you thinking. Most of us believe that self-indulgence is the key to satisfaction. Take what you can, when you can, because it may not come back around. If they have it, you need it. If you can't afford it, put it on that magic plastic and defer the payments as long as possible. This is what our culture teaches, and our sin selves have digested this doctrine so long our bellies

> HIS SELF-CONTROL SATISFIED OUR DEBT OF SIN, AND NOW WE LOVE HIM FOR IT.

are bloated. Our world preaches, "getting is everything," but I've met people who have nothing whose souls are happier than people who have everything.

Jesus used self-control to keep himself on the cross.

His motivation came from his love for the Father and for us (John 14:31). His self-control satisfied our debt of sin, and now we love him for it. His self-control produced satisfaction in us. Sadhana used her love for Jesus to practice self-control as she cleaned a man's rotting gangrene. Her self-control satisfied the man's need of compassion and her need to be successful as a nun. Take a minute to imagine Sadhana's satisfaction as she exclaimed, "Mother, I cleaned him!"

When has self-control brought satisfaction to your life? Now, let's look at how self-control brought satisfaction to King David.

DAVID AND SAUL IN THE CAVE

After David defeats Goliath, he marries Saul's daughter and becomes best friends with his son. He also becomes the king's right-hand man in battle. "Whatever Saul sent him to do, David did it so successfully that Saul gave him a high rank in the army. This pleased all the people, and Saul's officers as well" (1 Samuel 18:5). But one day, after a great victory, Saul's heart turns against David. The women come to greet King Saul, dancing and singing, "Saul has slain his thousands, and David his tens of thousands" (1 Samuel 18:7). Jealous thoughts twirl through Saul's mind. "They have credited David with tens of thousands, but me with only thousands. What more can he get but the kingdom?" (1 Samuel 18:8). Unable to control his envy, Saul plots to kill his son-in-law, who flees for his life.

It is under these circumstances where we find David and a band of loyal men hiding in a cave. Saul and his three thousand bounty hunters are hot on David's trail when Saul stops to relieve himself in the very cave where David is hiding. Concealed by the darkness, David's loyal men try to convince him that the Lord led Saul into the cave because it was time for David to kill him. Surely David's sin self wants to take Saul's life, but his redeemed self takes a section of the king's robe instead. After resisting this temptation, David rebukes his men, "The LORD forbid that I should do such a thing to my master, the LORD's anointed, or lift my hand against him; for he is the anointed of the LORD" (1 Samuel 24:6).

If this were a scene from an action movie, we'd all be silently screaming, "Kill him before he kills you!" Why didn't David kill a man who had been hunting him for years? We find the answer when David explains himself to Saul,

> See, my father, look at this piece of your robe in my hand! I cut off the corner of your robe but did not kill you . . . I have not wronged you, but you are hunting me down to take my life. May the LORD judge between you and me. And may the LORD avenge the wrongs you have done

to me, but my hand will not touch you. As the old saying goes, "From evildoers come evil deeds," so my hand will not touch you. (1 Samuel 24:11-13)

Let's get personal for a minute. Have you ever seen a leader fall? Perhaps a hero, pastor, parent, mentor, or someone you admired? How did you feel? Did you think, *How could they do that to themselves, to me, to everyone, to God?* Perhaps you even determined, "I'll never be like them." But perhaps after your moment of judgment, a little compassion and fear of the Lord kicked in, and you realized anyone can fall from any position.

Maybe, just for a minute in that cave, David considered taking Saul's life. But then compassion and fear of the Lord kicked in, and he remembered the old saying, "From evildoers come evil deeds." Perhaps David stopped because he knew the same evil that had invaded Saul's soul could poison his as well. Compassion and fear of the Lord forced him to slice the robe instead of Saul's throat. Self-control helped David trust the Lord to give him the kingdom instead of murdering to take it. Self-control gave David a clear conscience instead of a mind full of doubt and hatred.

If we want to love God more than our position, we have to remember that growing up is a posture, not a position. We have to make ourselves small so that God can do big things, and we have to remember that self-control is the key to satisfaction. Finally, we need to see sincerity as the strength of our story.

MR. SHERMAN

I have a hard time staying on this winding path through Sequoia National Forest because my eyes just won't look down. These trees have watched our world for thousands of years, and I feel so very small beneath them. My feet pause below the oldest and biggest tree in the world, the General Sherman. He stands out even though he's not the tallest or most pristine. Scars at his base prove he survived a fire. Green growth sprouts from what seems dead. A storm stole his top, preventing vertical growth, but his bark continues to expand, making his volume the biggest in the world.

My son, Joseph, cranes his neck, also impressed by Mr. Sherman. His curious voice speaks, "I wonder what will happen when he finally collapses under his own weight." The homeschool mom inside replies, "That will be a sad day indeed." I expect him to agree, but his reply matches his second-child perspective. "Not to the second biggest tree in the world. It will be a happy day for him." Giggle.

General Sherman is the oldest and biggest, but his height was stagnated in a storm. Does he feel like a failure? Is he frustrated by his lack of progress? Is he intimidated by the trees towering over him? What would he say if he had a voice? Would he tell us the secret to becoming the biggest or greatest? Would he explain how he survived the fires and blights that destroyed the younger and weaker trees?

Oh no! General Sherman is too wise. Sequoias have shallow root systems, so their height is their biggest weakness. Sherman lost his height suffering through a storm, but he's learned to thrive nonetheless. He no longer grows in height, but in width. He lost his position as the tallest, but his weighty base has helped him focus on his posture. The General isn't obsessed with his reputation. He knows he's not standing in his own strength, but by the grace of his creator. General Sherman knows what it means to stay small in his position. When his time to fall to the ground comes, he knows another tree will grow in his place because life isn't about him.

This is a sweet picture of The General. But what if Mr. Sherman took pride in his position, and then fell prostrate to the ground? Would you believe he got what he deserved? What if he knocked everyone down to elevate himself, but other trees started surpassing him? Would your distaste for Mr. Sherman make you cheer for the underdog? What if his prominence made him old and bitter, and then he suffered a great loss? Would you want to pick him up, or would you assume he'd loved himself quite enough for all of us?

If we let a little compassion and fear of the Lord come into our hearts, I think we'd have to admit we all love ourselves too much sometimes. When we see this ugly side of us, how do we make ourselves small? This is when we have to decide that sincerity is the strength of our story.

DAVID AND THE LAMB STORY

I wish I could tell you David loved Jesus more than his position during his entire life, but he didn't. Later in life, he used his influence to have an affair with another man's wife. When she became pregnant, he had the man killed. Obviously, this didn't please God, and since David covered up his behavior instead of repenting, God sent a prophet to confront him. The prophet, Nathan, broke David's heart with this story:

> There were two men in a certain town, one rich and the other poor. The rich man had a very large number of sheep and cattle, but the poor man had nothing except one little ewe lamb he had bought. He raised it, and it grew up with him and his children. It shared his food, drank from his cup and even slept in his arms. It was like a daughter to him.
>
> Now a traveler came to the rich man, but the rich man refrained from taking one of his own sheep or cattle to prepare

a meal for the traveler who had come to him. Instead, he took the ewe lamb that belonged to the poor man and prepared it for the one who had come to him. (2 Samuel 12:1-4)

At first, Scripture tells us that "David burned with anger against the man and said to Nathan, 'As surely as the LORD lives, the man who did this must die! He must pay for that lamb four times over, because he did such a thing and had no pity'" (2 Samuel 12:5-6). But then, sadly, Nathan said to David, "You are that man!" (2 Samuel 12:7).

SINCERITY IS STRENGTH

David looks a lot like the second version of General Sherman in this moment. He hears Nathan's story, points his finger, and judges the rich man, not knowing that this rich man was him. David indicted himself, but his heart didn't see his sin until Nathan broke his heart with this sweet, distressing story. Here's the truth: David could have used his position to cover up his sin. He'd already killed one man, why not two? If David had given into this impulse, he would have gone down in history as another one of Israel's evil kings. Instead, though, David let sincerity become the strength of his story.

God called David "a man after my own heart" (Acts

13:22). How could God say this about an adulterous murderer? A lesser king might have resented God for calling him out, said he was sorry, and begrudgingly obeyed God for the rest of his life. But the man after God's heart confessed, repented, and faithfully loved the Lord as the consequences of his sin tore his kingdom apart. David was a man after God's heart because he was willing to break his heart in order to re-align himself with God's. Sincerity was the strength of David's story because when faced with the choice of overriding God's conviction, he made himself a slave to God's will instead. David wasn't perfect, but he fought to keep God first.

Loving our position more than God is ugly, but we all do it. If we want to love God more, we have to accept that growth is a posture, not a position. We have to make ourselves small so that God can do big things, we have to believe that self-control is the key to satisfaction, and we have to accept sincerity as the strength of our story. Psalm 18:27 says, "You save the humble but bring low those whose eyes are haughty." When you're struggling to love Jesus more than your position, look for your humble moment. The way you respond to conviction determines whether you will pursue your sin self or your redeemed self.

> **WHEN YOU'RE STRUGGLING TO LOVE JESUS MORE THAN YOUR POSITION, LOOK FOR YOUR HUMBLE MOMENT.**

CHAPTER 5

I Love You More Than My Disappointment

"Hudson Taylor once said, 'We will all have trials.
The question is not when the pressure will come, but
where the pressure will lie. Will it come between us
and the Lord? Or will it press us ever
closer to his breast?'"
—Joanna Weaver, *Having a Mary Heart*
in a Martha World

JESUS AND THE SWING

Summer camp was a magical experience. Loving God, making friends, and bonding with newfound heroes—otherwise known as camp counselors—was everything a Christian teenage girl needed to boost her faith. But the last day of camp devastated my best friend and me. We sobbed all the way home wondering how we'd ever feel that excited about Jesus again.

We tried to prolong our camp high by spending the night together and reminiscing. Late one evening she got a phone call from her brother (a camp counselor who I may have had a crush on) asking if we'd like to raft the Ocoee River with a group of counselors. Smiles and silent squeals spun through the room like a tornado. Would a couple of teenage girls like to spend the day with their newfound college-aged friends? She took three deep breaths so she could reply with a calm and mature, "Sure."

Rafting day was everything I imagined. My face wore a permanent smile until my friend and her brother started sharing stories of their superhero father on the way home. Their memories should have warmed my soul. Instead, each happy memory felt like an arrow piercing my heart. I tried to share their enthusiasm, but my heart felt conflicted. Ashamed and embarrassed, I turned my attention to the window hoping something out there would keep me from ruining this perfect day. Why couldn't I enjoy this moment too? Something was wrong with me.

I searched, prayed, and waited, and then Jesus showed me. I was disappointed with God. Why didn't he answer my prayers and give me a good father? Have I not loved God enough? Does he not care about *me*? My real dad was a good guy, but our relationship stalled when he and my mom divorced when I was three. My second "father figure" led me into a five-year nightmare of sexual abuse. God helped me escape this relationship, and our family had a few good years with just my mom, my brother, and me, but I could tell that my mom was lonely. I had prayed that her next guy would love Jesus (and love us as a result), but we were three years into a new marriage by this point, and it seemed like this one would fail as well.

I'm tired of hoping. I'm tired of trying to believe "all things work together for good," I thought to myself. *They don't for me. I've repressed my desire for a good, good father, and now my friends have to rip my heart open with their fairytale life!*

These emotions, and so many more, left me feeling conflicted as we pulled into my friend's driveway. The ashamed part of me wanted to drive off with no goodbye, but the deep hurting part of me was longing to hear, "Are you okay?" I didn't know how to ask for help, so I lowered my head, opened my door, and headed straight for my car. I fumbled with my keys, hoping someone would cast an invitation to help my way, when I heard, "Sharie, are you okay?" Was I going to open my door and mumble, "I'm fine," or turn around and let them see a slobbering mess? I chose to become a mess. They surrounded me to pray, and through my weeping, I heard Jesus speak to me in a way I will never forget.

My mind's eye gazed toward a field covered in flowers surrounded by a rock wall. Beyond the wall was a wooden rope swing hanging from an oak tree. I ran toward the swing and planted myself on the seat. My feet pushed off the ground and started pumping when I felt a push from behind. Tilting my head back, I spied a figure who looked like the Jesus I'd always imagined. He pushed me forward, and when I swung back, he whispered, "Be at peace. I will be your Father. I am all you need."

His words were like a doctor giving me a shot. They had the medicine I needed, but they stung. The word "father" had become poison to my soul. This area of my life was so broken it seemed easier to remove it from my vocabulary and cut

> **WHEN WE SHUT JESUS OUT OF AN AREA OF OUR LIVES, OUR IDENTITY BECOMES MORE CONNECTED TO OUR HURT THAN OUR HEALER.**

off the hope valve. Jesus' words confused me and brought me out of my dream. Thanking my friends, I headed slowly to the car. On my drive home, I tried to figure out how to trust Jesus' words when they had the propensity to disappoint. I didn't come to a resolution, but I gave my heart permission to try to love Jesus more than my disappointment, hoping he'd prove trustworthy.

LOVING JESUS MORE THAN OUR DISAPPOINTMENT

How has disappointment visited you? Perhaps you didn't get that job or promotion. Maybe everyone else's dreams are raining from heaven while you're surrounded by a desert wasteland. It's easy to love Jesus more when things are going our way, but when life doesn't pan out as we expected it's tempting to cut Jesus out of the equation. But here's what I've noticed. When we shut Jesus out of an area of our lives, our identity becomes more connected to our hurt than our healer. We transfer our belonging from our faith to our feelings.

For too long I thought I had the right to be disappointed. If life dealt me a bad hand, I had the right to be bitter. If I made a mistake, I had the right to be mad at myself. But then I read 1 Peter 5:8: "Be self-controlled and alert. Your enemy the devil prowls around like a roaring lion looking for someone to devour." The sin self tells us we have the right to identify with our emotions. The redeemed self says, "be self-controlled and alert." Why does the redeemed self advise us to keep careful watch on our emotions? Because the devil is waiting and watching your reactions to see what ammunition he can use against you. Disappointment is like a nuclear bomb in his arsenal, so I want to show you three ways Jesus changed my perspective in order to transfer my belonging from my feelings to my faith. The first perspective change is the choice to chase the light or stay in the dark.

CHASE THE LIGHT OR STAY IN THE DARK

When I was little, if someone hurt my feelings, I'd run

to the safety of my bedroom closet and sing, "Nobody likes me. Everybody hates me. Guess I'll go eat worms. Big, fat, juicy worms. Long, slim, slimy worms. Oh, how they wiggle and squirm." Commiserating felt good for a quick minute, but I soon started to miss the people outside my dark prison. The light and noise traveled through the slats in the door, luring me into my mom's comforting arms.

When we're disappointed, we can choose to run to the dark closet of our minds or choose to chase the light. As you read these words in this "Christian" book, you probably know that the obvious choice is to chase the light. But you also probably know it's easier to know what you should do than to actually do it. Why do we commiserate in the dark more than we chase the light? Why are dark closets so addicting? Because disappointment is less like a word and more like a disease. If we don't recognize its presence, it will poison our emotions and taint our theology. Dark closets devour our faith and trick us into believing that Jesus is the source of our pain. Let me show you how lingering disappointment rots the soul.

I didn't know I was dissatisfied with God until my friend's family narratives penetrated through my bitter walls. As I listened to them, accusations slung through my mind: "God loves her more than you. If he loved you, he'd give you a life like hers. He's forgotten about you." Disappointment enticed me to envy her, resent

God, and alienate myself. When you hear accusations like this, be alert because the Enemy wants to devour you! This is your choice moment. Will you stay in darkness or chase the light?

I started to chase the light when I let my friends pray for me. Then, I was tempted to go back when I heard Jesus say, "Be at peace. I will be your Father." The darkness tried to lure me back by convincing me that Jesus didn't care about me. He wasn't answering my prayers correctly. I thought I needed a good father *here*, not in heaven. But Jesus was trying to move me past my disappointment. If he had been sitting across the table at a coffee shop, his words might have sounded like this: "Sharie, here's the reality. You may not experience the close, tender love of an earthly father, but I am with you always. I will adopt and take care of you. You need to make a choice: crawl into your miserable closet, or find the love you need in me."

> LOVING JESUS MORE THAN OUR DISAPPOINTMENT MEANS WE HAVE TO ACCEPT HIS ANSWERS TO OUR PRAYERS INSTEAD OF TRYING TO FORCE HIM TO GIVE US WHAT WE WANT.

Loving Jesus more than our disappointment means we have to accept his answers to our prayers instead of trying to force him to give us what we want. We must move forward when we want to mope. Simply put, we have to trust Jesus more than our feelings.

I hope this first step has brought you freedom. The

next step we have to take in our perspective shift is to trade in our magnifying glass for a wide-angle lens.

TRADE IN THE MAGNIFYING GLASS FOR A WIDE-ANGLE LENS

1. YOU ARE NOT ALONE

In Matthew, Jesus tells a story about a business owner who is going on a trip. Before the man leaves, he "entrusts" his wealth to three of his servants, hoping they will make his money work for him while he is away. Each one is given a different amount according to his ability, which means the owner believed that each one was capable of wise stewardship. However, when he returns, two made a profit while the other one, too scared to lose everything, buried his money in the ground (Matthew 25:14-30).

Confession: I'm a rule follower who leans a little more on the truth-and-justice side than the grace-and-mercy one. I'm more of a law-leaner than a grace-giver. So, it's always been hard for me to digest the fact that the owner gave the three workers different amounts. I know it was his money, and he had the right to do with it as he pleased, but I always wondered if the man with only one bag didn't feel like he got a fair shake. But then, my pastor Brad Cooper opened my eyes with this thought: "I imagine we are all the person in the middle. Someone will always have more, and someone will always have less." Brad's words helped solidify this spiritual truth. There will always be people in our lives who have an "easier" life (like my friend and her brother), but there will also always be people who've experienced far greater tragedy. In this world, normal and fair do not exist. There is no such thing as a "normal family" or "normal life." Each life contains its own degree of dysfunction and disappointment.

Therefore, we each have a choice. We can obsess and analyze our problems through a microscope or trade them in for a wide-angle lens.

Here's the difference. When you examine your problems under a microscope, they are enlarged and out of proportion. The sight line is limited and short-sighted. Your microscopic perspective deceives you into believing that you're alone in your suffering, your suffering is greater, and everyone else's life is more desirable. The wide-angle lens, however, expands your perspective, opening your eyes to the people around you. In fact, when your eyes aren't so narrowly focused, you will notice that each individual carries his or her own suitcase of setbacks. A broader scope may reveal that their life isn't as perfect as you first assumed. You might even discover that their situation is exponentially worse than your own. The first lesson the wide-angle lens teaches us is this: You

> WE CAN OBSESS AND ANALYZE OUR PROBLEMS THROUGH A MICROSCOPE OR TRADE THEM IN FOR A WIDE-ANGLE LENS.

are not alone. You are not the only one hurting or disappointed.

This isn't a message we want to hear, but it is a message we need. We need to understand that everyone is susceptible to disappointment so that we stop feeling sorry for ourselves. We need

A LINGERING SITUATION IS A LEARNING OPPORTUNITY.

to know that very few situations turn out the way we anticipate so that we don't identify ourselves as victims. No one can control or run away from disappointment. We can either manage the emotion or become manipulated by this monster.

The second lesson the wide-angle lens teaches us is this: A lingering situation is a learning opportunity.

2. A LINGERING SITUATION IS A LEARNING OPPORTUNITY

Lazarus was on his death bed when Mary and Martha sent this message to Jesus: "Lord, the one you love is sick" (John 11:3). Even though Mary, Martha, and Lazarus were three of his favorite people, Jesus didn't rush to rent the nearest donkey and beeline it for Bethany. He didn't immediately transport himself to Lazarus' bedside and heal his beloved friend. Scripture says, "although Jesus was very fond of Martha, Mary, and Lazarus, he stayed where he was for the next two days and made no move to go to them" (John 11:5-6, TLB).

Jesus lingered.

And then, "finally, after two days, he said to his disciples, 'Let's go to Judea . . . Our friend Lazarus has fallen asleep'" (John 11:7,11, TLB).

The microscopic view left the disciples confused. Why return to Bethany if Lazarus is just sick? Why risk their lives for a man who can recover on his own? But then Jesus clarifies that Lazarus has died, but it's a good thing he wasn't with him because his absence can help them believe.

When Martha heard of Jesus' arrival, she ran to him and exasperatedly cried, "If you had been here, my brother wouldn't have died" (John 11:21, TLB). Mary confesses something similar moments later. "If you had been here, my brother would still be alive" (John 11:32, TLB). Even outsiders asked, "This man healed a blind man—why couldn't he keep Lazarus from dying?" (John 11:37-38, TLB).

Can you hear their disappointment? Jesus was their friend. Wasn't he supposed to save them from death's devastation? From a microscopic view, Mary and Martha probably felt abandoned, disappointed, resentful, overlooked, and undervalued. Why would Jesus busy himself healing other people when his close friends needed him? Not only does Jesus abandon them during Lazarus' sickness, but he also misses the mourning and burial. He doesn't show up until Lazarus has been dead four days, he offers no apology, and he expects them to simply believe (John 11:25-26). Surely Jesus seemed inconsiderate in their microscopic perspective.

Watching his friends endure this test didn't give Jesus joy. His absence brought his loved one's intense pain for a season, but he had to wait, or their hearts wouldn't have been able to receive the lesson he needed to teach. As he stared into Mary's wondering eyes, tears came to his own; she didn't understand why the teacher had disappointed her.

It was time to open her perspective, though. It was time to show everyone that a lingering situation is often a learning opportunity.

Jesus' wide-angle view led him to linger away from Bethany. His timing didn't feel right to anyone else, but he was waiting for the *just-right time*. He waited for their desperation to rise. He waited until they couldn't believe in anything else *except* him. He had to teach them that he could raise the dead, just like Abraham believed God could raise his son, Isaac (Hebrews 11:19). Lazarus' resurrection wouldn't have come unless Jesus had lingered. He lingered so they could learn that he is the Lord of the living *and* the dead.

Jesus lingered.

Confession: When I'm in a season of suffering, I often hear myself wonder, *Is God playing a cruel trick on me?* Deep down, I know he's not, but it's tempting to believe that he is. After my hard season has passed, I remember that God's desire is never to disappoint, but always to help me develop. His lingering teaches me to climb above my situation to find my wide-angle view. It's hard to wait on God when he's waiting on us, but he won't move us forward until we're faithful in our current situation. I wonder what darkness you might need to leave in that closet or what microscopic perspectives you need to abandon so that you can move forward in your faith.

GOOD, GOOD FATHER

If you've ever built a house, you know it takes years before it feels like home. It took us seven years of hard labor to cover our rocky hill with grass, substantial shrubs, and flowers. We had just gotten the just-right paint, picture placement, and furniture to finally relax when Jesus asked us to move. Every cell in my being wanted to ignore him. Instead, our entire ministry team prayed about the decision, and after a tear-streaming meeting in November of 2013, we committed to move.

Our family immediately put our house on the market. I tried to keep things tidy and ready for *that* call from our realtor, but it never came. "Maybe God wants me to prove my faith," I thought. So, I packed, packed, and packed, creating a mountain of boxes in our living room to prove to Jesus (and myself) that I was ready and waiting . . . on *him* of course. Jesus didn't respond. For seven months, *no one* looked at our house (except a car full of nuns . . . which is a story in and of itself). I was waiting for God to do the amazing, but two months from our move date, a large part of my soul had given up. I walked into church feeling unnoticed and abandoned. My angry heart could hardly sing, so I was relieved to sit for the message. As Kaleb White preached about Jesus calming the storm on the sea, I wondered why Jesus wasn't calming mine. *Jesus, we need to sell our house to buy a new home. If we don't sell, who will manage our home here? Why have you taken care of everyone on our team* except *us? Don't you love us? Why are you not honoring our faith?* I tuned out. My frustrated and arrogant heart refused to listen to the sermon. I'd heard this message *in* Israel, sailing *on* a boat, *on* the Sea of Galilee. Nothing new here.

But then, Kaleb's message penetrated my stubbornness. Kaleb said, "Jesus left them in the boat to row until it was almost dawn while he prayed on the mountain." I realized the mountain Jesus was praying on is located just beside the Sea of Galilee. Therefore, the disciples were probably within Jesus' line of sight. This means Jesus chose to pray and watch the disciples row three to four miles against a storm of tidal waves and wind instead of rescuing them? He could have ended their misery, but he chose to linger? Was Jesus choosing to linger while we struggled through this house sale?

Tears dripped onto my Bible as I searched for an answer in Mark 6:51-52: "Then [Jesus] climbed into the boat with them, and the wind died down. They were completely amazed, for they had not understood about the loaves; their hearts were hardened."

"For seven months I've been packing boxes, rowing my boat *for you*, Jesus. You ask me to trust you, but you aren't acting on my behalf. Why aren't you helping me?" As I prayed, I realized my heart was hard, just like the disciples. I didn't understand the loaves any more than the disciples. I wasn't *resting* in Jesus' provision, but working *for* it. Embarrassed and deflated, I pleaded like a child, "Jesus, can you just help us? I give up."

The next week, we got three phone calls to show the house. On Friday of that week, a man stood on our deck and said, "I want to buy this house, and I'm willing to pay cash." Shocked, Clayton said, "Well, would you like to see the inside of the house?" By Saturday at 10:00 a.m. the contract was signed with a large amount of earnest money. As if this miracle wasn't enough, God started raining more from heaven. Check this out. Because closing was so close to our five

> I WASN'T RESTING IN JESUS' PROVISION, BUT WORKING FOR IT.

weeks of summer camp, we couldn't move out immediately. So the new owners let us live *in their house* for two months rent free, and they paid cash for all of our farm equipment and most of our furniture so that we didn't have to store it. The last miracle was the best of all. The fiancé of the man who looked at the house wasn't a Christian. She came to a camp service one night, met Jesus, and is now in seminary.

It isn't easy to believe God is good when we feel alone

or misinterpret God's lingering. Looking back on the house sale, I understand his timing. He waited so we could live in our own home until the day we moved. God's lingering also allowed another ministry family with a small child (they sold their house in four days) to have a home in our basement. We felt alone, but God's lingering proved to be the perfect provision.

WILL YOU BELIEVE YOU'RE A DADDY'S GIRL?

When Jesus returned to Bethany, he said to Martha, "But didn't I tell you that you will see a wonderful miracle from God if you believe?" (John 11:40) Martha's microscopic view never imagined Jesus would give life to a man who had been dead for four days. But he did. She didn't understand the miracle because she wasn't looking through Jesus' wide-angle lens. She thought the stone on Lazarus' tomb protected her from death, but it was the only thing separating Lazarus from life. Mary and Martha rowed through a terrible storm to understand that Jesus was able to defeat death.

Are you rowing through a storm of disappointment right now? If so, please know he has not abandoned you, and he is not lingering because he doesn't care. Jesus is up on the mountain praying while you row. *He has to linger so you can learn.* He is waiting and watching the storm until our hearts reach their just-right condition to receive his rescue.

The practical miracles from our house sale were pretty amazing, but the most wonderful miracle was my heart change. During my season of packing boxes, I attended our church's Father's Day service. Although my daddy issues aren't as raw as they used to be, I still struggle. During the

> **HE IS WAITING AND WATCHING THE STORM UNTIL OUR HEARTS REACH THEIR JUST-RIGHT CONDITION TO RECEIVE HIS RESCUE.**

service, they played a tender video of fathers with their families. The last picture was a little girl sitting on her father's lap wearing a shirt that read, "Daddy's Girl."

Disappointment squeezed this bitter statement from my heart: "I'll never wear a shirt like that." The moment flashed through my mind when Jesus sold our house, and I heard God say to me, "Sharie, I want you to buy a 'Daddy's Girl' shirt, and then I want you to wear it to declare that you are mine! Think about it. What kind of earthly father could have sold your house for the just-right price at the just-right-time?"

I made my shirt, and I wear it proudly.

Disappointment is an emotion that keeps us from loving Jesus more and understanding that God is good. His plan may not always line up with ours, but we can trust him to take us down roads we don't understand because he will always provide the faith we need to find our wide-angle-view. I never thought I would call myself a Daddy's Girl. But on Father's Day 2015, God proved he could do for me what no earthly father ever could. What area of disappoint-

> **DISAPPOINTMENT IS AN EMOTION THAT KEEPS US FROM LOVING JESUS MORE AND UNDERSTANDING THAT GOD IS GOOD.**

ment is God asking you to love him more through so that he can develop you into the woman he knows you can be?

CHAPTER 6

I Love You More in My Forgiveness

---

*"People who have failed are more generous with their
compassion, more extravagant with their love,
and less inhibited in their expressions of both."*
— Bob Goff, Foreword of *People of
the Second Chance*

JACKIE

Jackie loses her father at the tender age of nine. She doesn't know how to pick up her heart, and neither does her mom. Jackie's mom begins to take out her emotional frustration on her little girl, beating her with broomsticks and verbally pounding her into the ground. One night, Jackie is quietly sleeping when something startles her awake. Her mom is threatening to kill her by holding a cold knife across her neck. Desperate, Jackie decides to report her mom to the authorities hoping this dark cloud will pass. But speaking up is only the beginning of a new storm. For the next few years, Jackie is tossed from one toxic foster home to another.

Her storm seems like it is here to stay, until one day her brother and his wife invite her to live with them. Is the sun starting to shine on her life? Jackie is proud to live with her own family in her own home. And soon a new family member arrives—a new nephew! Jackie and the boy cultivate a strong bond. After eight months, Jackie's brother and his wife want to resume their social life, but their infant son is too consuming. They hand over their parenting responsibilities to Jackie. This is a tall job for a sixteen-year-old, but Jackie agrees because she loves her nephew.

One night, she and the baby are home alone. The little boy is incessantly screaming, crying, and sobbing. As she rocks him back and forth, tears come to her eyes as panic beats beneath her chest. Jackie can't pacify the little guy, and she is starting to lose control of herself. She *needs* him to be quiet, but he won't, and now he's getting too heavy to hold. Suddenly her emotions snap, and like a zombie, she stretches out her arms and watches as he rolls down toward the floor. The floor thuds when he hits it, and Jackie expects him to wail, but an eerie silence follows instead.

She is momentarily relieved and thinks to herself, "He's going to be okay." But when she kneels to check on the small bundle, she notices his closed eyes and still chest. Dark clouds hover over her soul as she realizes the instant his crying ceased, so did his heart. Jackie spends the next five years wishing her life away in juvenile detention.

"I'm a murderer. If I could kill such an innocent and pure baby, I deserve to die."[13] Hatred for herself becomes so deep that her release from jail doesn't produce an ounce of emotional freedom. She trades a physical prison for an emotional one.

Empty, Jackie tries to fill her void with sex, drugs, and partying. She is moving from shelter to shelter with her four kids when she meets someone special. A lady from a food drive invites her to a church service. Jackie rejects her offer right away just knowing that church people, and especially God, reject people like her. She doesn't belong in church, but the lady's persistence changes Jackie's mind. She survives one service, and afterwards, the desire to return won't go away. The chance to be loved by God keeps tugging at her heart, so she starts to attend regularly. Jackie is scared, skeptical, and shy, but at her just-right time, hope seeps into her heart as she hears the pastor say, "Jesus loves all his children, and there is no sin he won't forgive."

Maybe he will forgive me, Jackie thinks.

Finally, on August 21, 2011, Jackie hears Jesus speak to her. "It's time to stop. It's time to stop running."

This moment changes the direction of Jackie's life forever. She describes it like this: "Right then and there I invited Jesus into my life. I knew that he loved me despite who I was and my dark past. As messed up as I was, I knew I was totally forgiven, and there was a chance for me. He did it for me, and he can do it for you."[14]

GOD'S FORGIVENESS IS FINAL

The day her nephew died, a part of Jackie died as well. Because she'd taken his life, she believed hers should be taken too. Her sin self tried to alienate her from God by tricking her into believing that Jesus would forgive anyone but *her* and any sin but *her sin.*

Have you believed a similar lie? I have. Very often, I've found that the hardest person to forgive is myself. We desire forgiveness, but we don't feel like we have the right to receive it. We believe God forgives most of our sins, but maybe not *that one.*

I'm tired of believing this lie, so let's fight it with the truth. Scripture says, "God made him who had no sin to be sin, so that we might become the righteousness of God" (2 Corinthians 5:21). Through Jesus, the forgiveness of sins is proclaimed to you. Through him, everyone who believes is set free from every sin. In other words, God's forgiveness is final. Jesus doesn't pick and choose which of your sins are covered in his blood and which aren't because he conquered *every sin* on the cross. If we believe otherwise, we cheapen the message of his death and resurrection. When Jesus rose from the dead, did he conquer all of hell, death, and the grave, or just part of it? Does Jesus' blood cover *all* your sins? Yes.

My first glimpse of Jackie was in a worship service. I didn't yet know her story, but as she sang, I could tell she needed to love Jesus, and she needed him to love her back. I was jealous of her joy. It wasn't the bad kind of jealousy; it was the motivational kind—a godly jealousy that challenged me to connect with Jesus on a deeper level. You see, Jackie's life from the

> **IF WE WANT TO LOVE JESUS MORE IN OUR FORGIVENESS, WE HAVE TO RECEIVE HIS COMPLETE FORGIVENESS.**

outside hadn't seemed very good, but during this moment of worship, she was obsessed with absorbing all the goodness Jesus was sending her way. She believed that everything needing forgiveness in her life had been forgiven. And her redeemed self fights to help her believe this truth every day.

If we want to love Jesus more in our forgiveness, we have to *receive* his complete forgiveness, believing that his blood covers our sin in full, not in part. God's forgiveness is final; everything we ask him to forgive is forgiven. Maybe you haven't experienced this kind of forgiveness from your friends, family members, or even your church, but our Lord's forgiveness is final and countercultural.

GOD'S FORGIVENESS IS COUNTERCULTURAL

When I go home for Christmas, my Nanny always says something like this: "It's good to see you, honey. I don't know why the Lord is letting me linger in this world when I'm ready to go to my real home with Jesus and your Granddaddy, but I need you to tell me if there's anything you want me to leave you in case I don't last much longer. We have to divide my belongings now because with fifty family members, this place is going to be a madhouse when I die."

When Nanny first started the tours around her home so that I could stake my claim, the entire process felt awkward and disrespectful. She is one of my heroes, so honoring her life is more important to me than getting her stuff. Since my grandmother does this every time I visit, I've decided this is her way of welcoming me home. I've learned to giggle about it and get with the program.

Jesus tells a story in Luke 15 about a young man who treated his father quite the opposite. Something created a chasm between the boy and his father, which the boy considered beyond repair. He decided to leave, taking his father's inheritance prematurely. Let's look at the story through the eyes of the father.

The man of the house walks in the door from a hard day's work. His youngest son meets him in the doorway before he can catch a shower and grab a bite to eat. "Dad, I'm done with you, your religion, your people, and this stale village. I'm going to make a life for myself somewhere else, and I don't plan on ever returning or seeing you again. Can you give me whatever money you would give me when you die so I can start my new life?"

The man of the house is devastated, but not surprised. His son has already caused him many worrisome and sleepless nights, so he looks in his son's eyes and pleads, "Let's not talk about this now, son. I'm tired. We'll get to it in the morning."

The father walks into his bedroom, and falling backward onto his bed with tears rolling down his cheeks, he decides to love his boy one last time by granting his request. There's no way to measure the future value of his inheritance, so the next morning, the father gives the younger son half of his current possessions. The amount is overly generous, but maybe it will soften his child's heart. Cash in hand, the son heads for the door, ignoring his father's open arms and offering him a cold shoulder instead.

According to Jewish custom, by asking for his inheritance prematurely, the boy is declaring to his father (and the entire community), "You are dead to me." Even after insult, the father refuses to hate or become bitter, though. From this day on, every night, the father comes home from work, takes a shower, eats dinner, and sits on the front porch praying for his son's return. A long time passes. The man wonders if he's an old fool to hope, but he can't resist his prayer time on the porch. And then, on one certain night, a chill fills the air as the sun is setting. This is his normal cue to retire for the evening, but as he rises from his seat and reaches for the door, he notices the form of a young man on the horizon. The hopeful father shoves his feet in his boots and sprints toward the hill trying to reach his son. Undeterred by his son's filth, the father gives his son a powerful embrace that almost knocks the skeleton of a boy to the ground. The boy must have suffered much while he was away, so the father smothers his baby with kisses. It's time to celebrate. His son who was lost is now home!

What's your automatic reaction when someone wrongs you? To be honest, my sin self's reaction is vengeance or payback. Because forgiveness isn't my automatic reaction, I project this same response onto my Father in heaven. But God's kingdom isn't directed by our feelings or cultural norms, but by the character of our creator. God isn't eager to punish us. "Instead, he is patient with you, not wanting anyone to perish, but everyone to come to repentance" (2 Peter 3:9).

When Jesus shared this parable of the father and his lost son, he was opening his audience's eye to the true nature of God's love. In Jewish culture, reconciling with a son who blatantly dishonored his father was insulting, detestable, and unforgivable. In Jesus' story, the son not only slapped his father's face, but also disrespected the entire community. The law stated that the community had the right to punish and turn the son away, but the compassionate father ran to his son's rescue. The father's kiss actively reinstated his son into the family, and no one had the right to override this decision.

One of my favorite verses is Proverbs 16:15: "When a king's face brightens, it means life; his favor is like a rain cloud in the spring." When Jesus absorbed and overcame our sin, he removed the wrath we deserved. When your King in heaven looks on you, his face is bright and smiling. Everything in your life that needs forgiveness has been forgiven. God is not holding your sin against you, so relax. Look up and let his favor pour over you. Drink his countercultural forgiveness; it is final, and it is generous.

GOD'S FORGIVENESS IS GENEROUS

Trish put her faith in Jesus when she was seven years old in the sanctuary of her home church. Her heart was full of giggles, and her hands were ready to serve Jesus wherever and whenever she could plug in at church. She loved God sincerely until she learned of a few scandals among the church leadership. Disillusioned by their sin, she started dabbling in scandalous behavior herself, skipping school, lying to her parents, "dating," and partying. She found out she was pregnant the summer before her senior year. Not ready for a child, the father asked her to have an abortion, but she couldn't follow through with it. He left because Trish chose the baby over him, and Trish felt abandoned.

Her daughter was still tiny when Trish met a man who adored both her and her daughter. They fell in love, and life seemed to be moving in the right direction until her boyfriend decided to join the military, and Trish found out they had a baby on the way. Her new love had a change of heart, so they broke off the engagement. She felt abandoned again but decided to give birth to her baby boy.

Motherhood isn't easy for any woman, but being a single mom sometimes left her feeling defeated. Trish couldn't keep up with the bills, and the guilt of not being able to give her kids a good father ate her alive. She started dating and ended up pregnant, *again*. She was sure she'd never be worthy of another man's love. She felt insufficient, broken, trashy, and used up. Raising three children was a storm she couldn't weather alone, so she decided to get an abortion.

Trish hoped no one would protest the day she showed up, but they did. She was condemned as they screamed, "Baby killer! Murderer, Sinner!" Some people offered help, but her shame led her past them to a seat beside the door inside the clinic. She thought she might change her mind, but she had no time before the nurse came to escort her to a procedure room. "Are you sure you want to go through with this?"

"Yes," Trish answered. She lay on the table, pleading for God's forgiveness the entire time. When it was over, she felt empty inside. She couldn't believe she had willingly agreed to end a child's life. Her child's life. She somehow felt like she had out-sinned the grace she'd received when she was seven and that the sins she'd committed after she was saved weren't covered by Jesus' grace. She could ask his forgiveness, but could she really blot out that stain and be freed from that sin? Just as she had been abandoned by her children's fathers, she thought maybe Jesus didn't want her anymore.

But this isn't the end of Trish's story. In Trish's own words, "Jesus knew I was hurting, and he was not okay with that."

"She soon married a good man who adopted her two children. The two not only got involved in church, but Trish also became a staff member. She soon learned that the church planned to transform the clinic where she'd gotten her abortion into a place for children. No one knew her story, and she planned to keep it hidden. But when Trish went to the grand opening, she "walked around the room where she had ended her child's life, and Jesus whispered to her in that moment, 'It is finished.' She knew right then that he had not only redeemed her in her heart, but also the building where her sin had taken place. She could never out-sin the grace of God. God's grace was sufficient for the worst thing she had ever done."[15]

Trish believed a lie you might find familiar: God is a reluctant forgiver. Your sin self wants to keep you shackled to your sin. It whispers these lies in your ear:

- "If people really knew you and what you've done, they'd never accept you."
- "Your sins are too big, too shameful, and too costly to give to Jesus."
- "Jesus loved you enough to pay for your sins, but he doesn't like you."

But your redeemed self preaches, "For God so loved the world that he gave his one and only Son, that whoever believes in him shall not perish but have eternal life" (John 3:16). God's "love is patient, love is kind. It does not envy, it

> GOD'S FORGIVENESS COVERS EVERY SIN COMPLETELY WITH NO RECORD OF WRONGS.

does not boast; it is not proud. It does not dishonor others, it is not self-seeking, it is not easily angered, it keeps no record of wrongs. Love does not delight in evil but rejoices with the truth. It always protects, always trusts, always hopes, always perseveres" (1 Corinthians 13:4-7).

God's forgiveness covers every sin completely with no record of wrongs.

God forgives because he is generous, not because we deserve it. We are forgiven because he is loving. If we reject his forgiveness because we don't feel like we deserve it, we're trying to earn a love we've already received. It's like trying to pay your grandmother back for your Christmas present. She won't accept it, and neither will Jesus. Jesus already absorbed the wrath you're placing on yourself. Forgiveness is yours if you're ready to receive it. Whatever your inner struggle might be, please don't let your sin self, based on your emotions, convince you that God is a reluctant forgiver. God will never stop extending the grace you seek.

THE ELEPHANT'S TRUNK

In 1997, Clayton and I took a team on an excursion to the pink palace in Jaipur, India. The bus screamed with excitement when the guide announced, "You will be touring the castle and riding painted elephants!" When we arrived, we unloaded and scaled a few flights of stairs to an open platform. We were standing face-to-face with the majestic animals. I became so mesmerized by the painted designs on their skin that I didn't hear our team member screaming beside me. While I was dazed, an angry elephant started swinging its trunk back and forth almost knocking one of our girls off the two-story platform! The conductor regained control of the animal before disaster could strike, but if the animal's trunk had hit her, her injuries would have been terminal. Our friend was not the source of the elephant's misery, but his misdirected frustration almost ended her life.

Elephants aren't our enemy, but an angry one can become dangerous. Emotions aren't our enemy either, but if we let the poison of a bad experience burrow deep into our heart, it can contaminate the soil of our soul. If we don't pursue healing, our pain becomes a ticking time bomb waiting to explode. James 5:15 says, "The prayer offered in faith will make the sick person well; the Lord will raise him up. If he has sinned, he will be forgiven." Why do we stuff away sins that God promises to heal?

We know forgiveness will heal our hurt, but we're afraid, so we wait. What are we waiting for? Do we think an unquenchable desire to forgive is going to magically appear? Deep-hearted forgiveness is rarely accompanied by a good feeling. More often, forgiveness isn't a feeling, but a fight. If we're going to love Jesus more in our forgiveness, we may have to fight for it.

FORGIVENESS IS WORTH THE FIGHT

When I asked Jesus to forgive and save me from my sins, the moment felt a little magical. When I was a young Christian, I thought forgiveness was always accompanied by a magical feeling. I thought forgiveness worked like a Band-Aid. Place it over your wound, and wait for it to heal. But most often, forgiveness isn't easy, and it certainly doesn't work like magic. Wounds of the soul don't heal without hard work. I want to give you some tools to make forgiveness work for you. Let's look at two different kinds of forgiveness.

1. FORGIVENESS THAT RESULTS IN RECONCILIATION

The most satisfying kind of forgiveness is the one that results in a restored relationship. In this kind of forgiveness, two people place enough value on their relationship to invest the time and energy needed to keep it healthy. In this kind of relationship, we will most often *feel* like forgiving because we either have a close bond already or have a deep-seated desire to keep the relationship alive.

Yesterday morning, my son and I had an argument that ended in a tense resolution. I woke up this morning feeling like I needed to repent because if I'd used more self-control, the argument wouldn't have been so intense. I sat down at breakfast, looked into my son's eyes, and said, "I'm sorry I lost my temper yesterday. I've been stressed; however, that's no excuse. It wasn't your fault, and I love you too much to treat you that way. Do you forgive me?"

"Yes, Mama. I shouldn't have been so hardheaded. Please forgive me too."

His forgiveness was humbling, but it was fairly easy because I knew my son's heart. I've also had forgiveness conversations that lasted more than an hour and took a lot of snot and tears before there was resolution. Sometimes we choose to forgive because being right isn't as important as making things right with our friend or loved one.

When I need to forgive a friend or family member, I remind myself that I will always be surrounded by imperfect people, so I have a lifetime of forgiveness ahead of me. I will have to forgive them, and they will have to forgive me back. We forgive others because we've been forgiven. We don't have the right to hold people's sins against them any more than they have the right to hold our sins against us. "It is probably better to forgive too much

> **WE FORGIVE OTHERS BECAUSE WE'VE BEEN FORGIVEN.**

than to forgive too little. Grace can afford a bit of over-spending."[16]

2. FORGIVENESS THAT RESULTS IN RELIEF

Sometimes a relationship cannot (or should not) be reconciled, so we use the tool of forgiveness to heal our heart. In this kind of forgiveness, you are the only one forgiving for two reasons: the other person is unwilling to work on the relationship, or they pose a threat to your emotional health. We use this kind of forgiveness in abusive relationships (physical, mental, or emotional) or in relationships that are unresolved. This kind of forgiveness is used to heal our heart from an offense rather than to restore a relationship.

HOW TO CHOOSE BETWEEN RESTORATION AND RELIEF

Joseph is one of my favorite people in the Bible because he encountered many difficult situations, and though he could have chosen bitterness, he chose to overcome instead. His family makeup was dysfunctional, to say the least. Jacob, his father, had two wives, Leah and Rachel, who each had her own servant, Zilpah and Bilhah. This is significant because each of these women bore children by Jacob, which caused as much dissention among their children as you might imagine. Rachel was Jacob's true love, so her children, Joseph and Benjamin, became his favorites. Jacob's special love for Joseph made his brothers envious, so they plotted to kill Joseph. Instead, though, they ended up selling him to a slave master. After decades of slavery and prison, Joseph finally caught a break when he interpreted a very significant dream for Pharaoh, thereby earning him a position as second-in-command in Egypt.

Pharaoh's dream gave Joseph the wisdom to prepare the nation of Egypt for seven years of famine, but many of the outlying villages were suffering greatly. Jacob and his family were among those suffering, so Jacob sent ten of his eleven children to purchase food in Egypt. When the brothers arrived, they were oblivious to the fact that their long-lost brother was the governor. The last time they saw Joseph, he was a slave, and now all of a sudden, they were bowing before him. Joseph eventually forgave his band of brothers, but not without a fight. Let's look at the steps Joseph took to restore their relationship.

1. HE KEPT HIS DISTANCE

When Joseph's brothers showed up in the palace, he recognized them, but didn't automatically run to embrace them. In fact, Scripture points out that he "pretended to be a stranger and spoke harshly to them" (Genesis 42:7) and accused them of being spies. They claimed to be honest men seeking food, but Joseph was cautious to believe them. Surely he was surprised to see them, and since their treatment of him previously was so inhumane, he remained skeptical.

Proverbs 14:15 says, "A simple man believes anything, but a prudent man gives thoughts to his steps." When you wonder whether or not to forgive someone who has vi-

> **TRUE FORGIVENESS IS A DEEP WORK, NOT A RASH DECISION MOTIVATED BY GUILT.**

olated your trust, use caution. Give thought to your steps. Jesus doesn't expect you to leap into the arms of someone who has hurt you. If the word forgiveness is on the table, keep your heart and emotions in check and listen deeply. True forgiveness is a deep work, not a rash decision motivated by guilt.

2. HE TESTED THEM TWICE

Joseph didn't know if he should trust his brothers or not, so he decided to test them, twice. His emotions were up and down like a roller coaster as he decided how to test them first. He waffled back and forth, first demanding that one of them stay in prison, sending the others to retrieve Benjamin. But he ended up changing his mind, throwing the entire group in prison for three days and then sending everyone but Simeon home to fetch Benjamin. Simeon would remain a prisoner until they returned. Why was Joseph so determined to see Benjamin with his own two eyes? Maybe he wondered if his jealous brothers had also sold or killed Benjamin. Was his beloved brother alive?

The first test was prison. For the second, Joseph ordered his servants to hide the bags of silver (Jacob's pay-
ment for the grain) in each brother's grain bags so they
would look like thieves. Maybe Joseph wondered if im-
prisoning Simeon was a big enough ransom. They had
abandoned Joseph, so why not Simeon too? But if they
were truly honest men, they would return the silver and
bring Benjamin to Egypt.

I can only surmise the motives of Joseph's heart in
testing his brothers. But we do know these tests began
to show Joseph who his brothers had become. During
the test, Joseph overheard this conversation between his
brothers: "Surely we are being punished because of our
brother. We saw how distressed he was when he pleaded
with us for his life, but we would not listen; that's why this
distress has come upon us" (Genesis 42:21). They didn't
know Joseph was eavesdropping on their conversation,
but their words were true! They were being punished because of their brother. Joseph was causing them distress
because they did listen to him, and now he was trying to
figure out if they had changed. Their confession brought
tears to Joseph's eyes, but he still wasn't ready to open his
arms to them.

Proverbs 13:16 says, "All who are prudent act with
knowledge, but fools expose their folly." When we are trying
to forgive someone who has hurt us deeply, we have to determine which kind of forgiveness is best—one that brings
restoration to the relationship or one that brings personal

healing. In order to "act with knowledge," you may need to do some testing to determine if the other person or people are willing to walk through forgiveness with you. Do they want restoration, or just for you to let them off the hook? If you let a disingenuous fish off the hook, they repeatedly return unchanged. But a fish desiring restoration will leave satisfied and settled.

3.HE INVITED THEM INTO HIS HOME

The nine brothers, plus Benjamin, returned to Egypt with gifts for Joseph. They not only brought the test bags of silver, but a doubled amount as well. When Joseph saw Benjamin, he invited everyone to his house for dinner. Then, he looked at his beloved Benjamin and said, "'God be gracious to you, my son.' Deeply moved at the sight of his brother, Joseph hurried out and looked for a place to weep. He went into his private room and wept there. After he had washed his face, he came out and, controlling himself, said, 'Serve the food'" (Genesis 43:29b-31).

When Joseph saw Benjamin, he could not keep his brothers at arm's length anymore. They had done everything Joseph asked, so Joseph invited them into his home. He still held his identity back, though. Why was he still afraid? Perhaps he felt emotionally healthy before his brothers arrived and was hesitant to hurt again, so he still guarded his heart.

Proverbs 4:23 reads, "Above all else, guard your heart, for it is the wellspring of life." Guarding your heart isn't the same thing as closing it off. The ideal goal in a relationship is restoration unless that goal proves impossible. If someone comes your way, move toward them a little. Joseph took the risk of inviting his brothers into his home, but he hadn't yet let them into his heart. You don't have to take a big step, but be willing to take a cautious one. Don't become so afraid to forgive that you forget that bitterness hurts too.

4. HE TESTED THEM A THIRD TIME

After a good dinner and a good night's sleep, the brothers were ready to return home, but before they left, Joseph had one last test planned. His servant planted a silver goblet in Benjamin's sack. The band of brothers only traveled a short distance before Joseph's steward caught up with them and accused them of stealing. Confused, the brothers responded, "Why would we steal silver or gold from your master's house? If any of your servants is found to have it, he will die; and the rest of us will become my lord's slaves" (Genesis 44:8-9). A thorough search revealed the goblet in Benjamin's sack. Devastated, the brothers returned to Joseph's home and "*threw* themselves to the ground" as Judah plead for Benjamin's life. This is what he said: "Now then, please let your servant remain here as my lord's slave in place of the boy, and let the boy return with his brothers. How can I go back to my father if the boy is not with me? No! Do not let me see the misery that would come on my father" (Genesis 44:33-34).

Imagine with me.

Joseph holds his brothers at a distance, tests them three times, and shares a meal with them. Throughout these trials, they prove themselves trustworthy, genuine, and repentant. As Joseph watches Judah offer his life as a ransom, his heart melts. He realizes that the Judah who threw him in that cistern and sold him as a slave is not the same Judah standing before him now. In this moment, Joseph decides to remove the wall around his heart. He previously forgave his brothers for the sake of his health, but now he will give them access to his heart. Forgiveness for the sake of his health brought him relief, but his fight to forgive is now producing reconciliation in his heart.

5. HE GAVE THEM ACCESS TO HIS HEART

After Judah's confession, Joseph couldn't control his emotions any longer, so he sent the Egyptians away and confessed:

> Come close to me. I am your brother, the one you sold into Egypt! And now, don't be distressed and do not be angry with yourselves for selling me here because it was to save lives that God sent me ahead of you . . . So, then, it was not you who sent me here, but God. He made me father to Pharaoh, lord of his entire household and ruler of all Egypt . . . Then, he

threw his arms around his brother Benjamin and wept, and Benjamin embraced
him, weeping. And he kissed all his brothers and wept over them. Afterward his
brothers talked with him. (Genesis 45:4-
5,8, 14-15)

I wept with Joseph when I first read this story through
the eyes of forgiveness. He must have let a lot of bitterness
fall off his back to give his brothers permission to forgive
themselves. But by doing this, they all experienced freedom and thrived as a family settling in the most beautiful
part of Joseph's dominion.

Not all of our stories will end the same as Joseph's.
Our goal should always be restoration, but if you ever
feel unsafe opening your heart as you travel through the
above steps, pause at any given stage until you feel safe
moving forward. Wait to see if the person you're trying
to forgive initiates a for-
giveness step toward you.
If they do, perhaps your
relationship will result in

> HIS FORGIVENESS IS
> GENEROUS, AND FORGIVENESS
> IS NOT A FEELING, BUT A FIGHT.

reconciliation. But if you feel reconciliation is impossible,
let go of the bitterness for the sake of your own relief and
personal healing.

People often give the advice, "forgive and forget," but
realistically, some offenses last a lifetime. I like to live by
this principle instead: When you remember, every time

you remember, fight for forgiveness and watch God heal your heart. "God invented forgiving as a remedy for a past that not even he could change and not even he could forget."[17] If you want to love God more in your forgiveness, remember this: his forgiveness is final. His forgiveness is generous, and forgiveness is not a feeling, but a fight.

CHAPTER 7

I Love You More Than My Dreams

---

*"Serve the One who loves you with excellence. But
don't use him to serve your personal agenda. God is
not a means to an end. He is the end."*
— Holly Gerth, *You're Made
for a God-Sized Dream*

MY CALLING

I was twelve years old when God called me into ministry. I
was young and terrified. It wasn't an epic moment. Angels
didn't visit me from heaven with trumpets in hand. No,
I was just a little girl sitting on one of a hundred pews
in an enormous church sanctuary. I was surrounded by
towering white walls and windows that reminded me of
skyscrapers. As I stared at a statue of Jesus above the choir
loft, I remember feeling like everything was so perfect and
properly placed . . . except me.

I remember wondering why Jesus had asked me to serve him with my life. Timid, shocked, and confused, I responded, "What does a little girl like me have to offer you? What do you want me to do? Who will teach me? I don't think I can do this, but I want to!"

As a teenager, I had no clue what it meant to serve Jesus, so I did what I thought someone in ministry would do—Sunday school, youth group, weekly prayer meetings, Scripture memorization, and mission trips. I hoped this was good enough. I wasn't perfect, but I was willing.

I continued "working" on my ministry résumé in college: Five mission trips, consistent Bible reading, church most Sundays, leadership in my campus ministry, extra times of prayer and fasting, discipled by the campus pastor and his wife, and finally, dating an evangelist. I didn't intend for my spiritual walk to become a list of accomplishments, but it did. I was trying to prove to Jesus that I was worth his choosing. If you could have eavesdropped on my heart the day I graduated college, it probably sounded a lot like this, "God, I did it! Are you proud of me? I'm spiritually grown up and ready for my ministry now!"

When I was a little girl, someone told me, "Sharie, you're smart, and you have so much to offer. Don't settle for less than the best." These words lifted me out of tough childhood experiences, but they frustrated me during my first few years in ministry. You see, life had taught me that good performance should be rewarded with trophies, good grades, or recognition. I'd always been taught that the fulfillment of a dream was the key to importance and satisfaction. But the first year Clayton and I were married, we spent 320 days on the road. He ministered at different churches and events while I *watched*. I was content with my role the first year because I was just happy to see him every day, but a second year of the same made me wonder if I was "settling for less than the best." Surely "I had more to offer" than to serve as Clayton's full time cheerleader . . . I felt overlooked and undervalued. My feelings waffled back and forth between entitlement and shame. This is how it played out in my mind:

- **Entitlement:** God, *this calling* is a waste of my mind, abilities, and potential. Don't you remember all the time I've put in? Isn't it time for a little payback?!

- **Shame:** God, have I sinned or done something wrong? Haven't I been faithful to serve you and grow? Why aren't you giving me more? Do you love Clayton more than me?

I had to communicate my feelings to my husband, but I was scared he would perceive me as selfish or ungrateful. But I mustered the courage to start the conversation on the way home one evening. "When I meet people at these churches and events, they always ask, 'So, what do you do?' I detest this question because I want to say, 'Nothing! I follow my husband around like a little lost puppy. I watch him preach and then stand by while crowds of people line up to tell him how much he's changed their lives.' I want to vent and walk away, but I know they don't deserve my belligerent outburst. So I usually say, 'My husband and I travel together in ministry because we value our marriage. It would be impossible to make it work otherwise.'" And then I worked up the courage to ask Clayton, "When do you think I will be able to travel and speak instead travel and watch?"

A big, scary silence entered our car as my young, newly married, good-intentioned husband tried to formulate a response. He answered, "Well, Sharie, I can't just push you off on people." As you can imagine, this answer didn't translate well with me. I wasn't asking him to push me off on people. I wanted him to believe in me. The rest of our ride home was a long, drawn-out, heated "discussion."

This was a sore subject in our married life until we learned how to do ministry together. And even though Clayton's wording wasn't ideal, he was right. I thought marrying someone in ministry was God's way of rolling out the red carpet for my ministry, but it wasn't my just-right time. I wanted my

> IF I WANTED TO BE A DISCIPLE, I HAD TO GIVE UP WHAT I WANTED IN ORDER FOR GOD TO GIVE ME WHAT I NEEDED.

husband to be wrong, but he wasn't. God was still in the process of transforming me into who I needed to become before I could do what I dreamed. If I wanted to be a disciple, I had to give up what I wanted in order for God to give me what I needed. I wanted to be a leader, but he still needed me to follow.

THE "BE BEFORE DO" PRINCIPLE

In Matthew 19, a man asks Jesus, "Teacher, what good thing must I do to get eternal life?" (Matthew 19:16) They begin a theological discussion about goodness and the law, but Jesus soon moves past the superficiality to address the man's heart. He says, "'If you want to be perfect, go, sell your possessions and give to the poor, and you will have treasure in heaven. Then, come, follow me.' When the young man heard this, he went away sad, because he had great wealth" (Matthew 19:21-22).

This man seemed like he wanted eternal life. He seemed like he wanted to do good and obey God, but when Jesus asked him to give up what he loved the most, his money, to follow him, "the young man went away sad." In my opinion, this is one of the most tragic interactions in the Bible. The wealthy man was willing to *do* whatever Jesus commanded except *become* who he needed to be. His dream of financial stability and abundance kept him from loving Jesus more.

It's easy to point the finger and say, "He sure is greedy!" But loving a good dream, even a godly dream, more than Jesus is sinful too. We think we are loving Jesus more because the dreams we are pursuing are virtuous, moralistic, or upright. But if we're more in love with what we are pursuing than who we are becoming, we have a broken motivator.

When I was twelve years old, sitting on a pew in that enormous sanctuary, I didn't feel like I had anything to offer God. My unsophisticated faith couldn't fathom God's choosing *little ol' me*. Twelve years and a few accolades later, my motivation had changed. I traded my wonder for entitlement. I was convinced that all of my hard work for Jesus should have landed me my dream job in ministry. I had a broken motivator, and it tempted me to become proud of my accomplishments instead of humbled by my opportunity to serve. I resented being used instead of relishing in my usefulness.

EXAMINING YOUR MOTIVATOR

What is the condition of your motivator? Are you still waiting on a dream? If so, this is the perfect time to ask yourself, "Do I love Jesus more than this dream?"

James, the brother of Jesus, teaches us how to examine our motivator:

> Who is wise and understanding among you? Let them show it by their good life, by deeds done in the humility that comes from wisdom. But if you harbor bitter

envy and selfish ambition in your hearts, do not boast about it or deny the truth. Such 'wisdom' does not come down from heaven but is earthly, unspiritual, and demonic. For where you have envy and selfish ambition, there you find disorder and every evil practice. But the wisdom that comes from heaven is first of all pure, then peace-loving, considerate, submissive, full of mercy and good fruit, impartial, and sincere. Peacemakers who sow in peace reap a harvest of righteousness. (James 3:13-18)

This is my interpretation of James' words: Do good things, but examine why you are doing them. Is your heart humble, or are you serving yourself? If you're serving yourself, don't hide it or lie to yourself. Selfish intentions and proud deeds will corrupt your heart. If you want to be wise, repent

> **IF YOUR MOTIVATOR IS IN THE RIGHT PLACE, YOUR DEEDS WILL TALK FOR THEMSELVES AND CHANGE THE WORLD AROUND YOU.**

and set your heart on a path to serve from a place of purity, peace, and unbiased compassion for others. If your motivator is in the right place, your deeds will talk for themselves and change the world around you.

If you struggle with your motivator, please know

you're not alone! The conflict between our desire to serve and our aversion to self-denial is one of the biggest duplicities of the Christian life. We are all guilty. We say we love God and love others more, but when we're given the choice, we often don't. Why do you think we fail in the follow-through?

Just like the young man who couldn't forfeit his wealth, we're probably afraid of what we will lose. I've often wondered, "If I love Jesus more than my dreams, will I have to give them up?"

Letting go of selfish ambition is excruciating, but it is essential to following through. If you're having trouble with your follow-through, don't give up. I'm convinced that re-positioning our motivator is a maturity step every believer has to experience in order to love Jesus more

> LETTING GO OF SELFISH AMBITION IS EXCRUCIATING, BUT IT IS ESSENTIAL TO FOLLOWING THROUGH.

than herself. "Unfortunately, though we all applaud the thought of transformation, most of us don't appreciate the process that gets us there. To be transformed often means we have to change, and change often hurts."[18]

Twelve-year-old Sharie was amazed that Jesus would choose someone with no previous experience. Twenty-four-year-old Sharie was banking on her experience. I didn't begin public speaking until I was thirty. This waiting period is what *be before do* really looks like. Nothing in me wanted to wait, but I had a lot to learn. When I traveled with Clayton, I learned practical skills like:

- How to carry on conversations with complete strangers.
- How to communicate a message and tell a story.
- How to have compassion for people unlike me.
- How to be flexible with my life rhythms (eating, sleeping, time alone, time with people).

I also learned soul lessons like:

- The church doesn't always act like the church.
- The bright lights and applause of the people seem confidence-building and affirming, but they can also make you insecure and lonely.
- People criticize prematurely, and I'm called to handle them maturely.
- Saying yes to ministry means I'm saying no to my husband and children. I have to make choices to protect my family (even if people don't understand).
- You can't please everyone.
- A message isn't always for everyone, but it's always for someone.

Here's the cold, hard truth. Jesus was right to hold me back from my dreams because I wasn't secure enough in my relationship with him to begin public ministry in

1999. I was so busy trying to prove I was credible that I forgot *he* is my credibility. I was so busy chasing my good dream that I was blind to my broken motivator. In 1999, *my* ministry would have been just that, *mine*—more about my dreams than his kingdom.

What is your cold, hard truth? Is Jesus holding you back from your dream for a reason?

Many times in Scripture, the Pharisees believed they were building God's kingdom, but their crucifixion of Jesus proved they were more focused on their own. Once, after witnessing endless miracles, they asked Jesus to prove his identity by performing a miracle. This was Jesus' answer: "A wicked and adulterous generation asks for a sign! But none will be given it except the sign of the prophet Jonah. For as Jonah was three days and three nights in the belly of a huge fish, so the Son of Man will be three days and three nights in the heart of the earth" (Matthew 12:39-40).

The Pharisees demanded a sign, and when Jesus did not meet their demands, they walked away holding their belief hostage. As much as I don't want to be like these Pharisees, I know my heart has also put conditions on my love for Jesus. "Jesus, if you love me, show me! I don't want to give you everything if you're not going to make my dreams come true." This is the shameful cry of our sin self.

What happens in your heart when Jesus doesn't fulfill your dreams according to your strategy and timetable? When he doesn't give you what you want, do you withdraw your love? Do you transfer your affection to your pursuits? Are you loving your dreams more than Jesus?

If Jesus had performed a miracle for the Pharisees, would they have loved him more? No! Jesus had already given them endless opportunities to believe, but none of his signs captured their hearts. So he refused to

> IF JESUS GAVE US EVERYTHING WE ASKED FOR, WE WOULDN'T LOVE HIM MORE; WE'D LOVE OURSELVES, OUR DREAMS, AND OUR ACCOMPLISHMENTS MORE.

give them anything except "the sign of Jonah." Just like Jonah spent three days in the belly of the fish, Jesus would soon give himself over to death for three days and then rise again, offering eternal life to everyone who believes. This was Jesus' final (and greatest) proof that he was God. And this is our greatest proof that he loves us.

If Jesus gave us everything we asked for, we wouldn't love him more; we'd love ourselves, our dreams, and our accomplishments more. When we ask Jesus to give us our dreams to prove his love, we've lost sight of our greatest treasure—our relationship with him.

A woman with a working motivator invests in her spiritual health before her happiness. Loving Jesus more than our dreams is a not a one-time decision, but a lifetime commitment of continued dedication. Over and over, a woman with a working motivator dies to herself and becomes more alive in him. Dear Lord, help us! Save us from our sin selves and restore to us the joy of your salvation. Make us willing to obey you!

Have you lost sight of your greatest treasure? Don't lose heart. I've been where you are many times, so I want to give you two ways to reset your motivator.

RESET #1: CHOOSE HEALTH OVER HURRY

When I was six months pregnant, my Nanny said, "You know honey, you need to be careful because it's hard to lose that baby weight." I half-heartedly listened to her. I was young, sporty, and in that idealistic stage where you think nothing bad will ever happen to you. A few years after my last child, the weight remained, and I was frustrated. I started running a 5K three times a week thinking those pounds would just melt away. They didn't. I told myself I wasn't discouraged. I tried to convince myself I was okay with my body until I watched that advertisement for a magic weight-loss pill. If *that pill* melted *her* fat while she was eating *that,* what could it do for *me* if I keep up my 5K? I knew it was a get-rich scheme, but I was in a hurry to get my body back, so I obsessed over the sales video. I watched it over and over, so many times that I finally caved in. I bought those ridiculous pills. Oh, yes, I did. But I'm not proud. They did not work. In the beginning, I lost five enormous pounds, but then I slid right back to my post-baby weight.

When we want to lose weight, a magic pill or shake promising an hourglass figure is more tempting than a two-year eating-and-exercise plan because it's quick and easy. But deep down, we know short cuts don't produce the same results as hard work over time. I've lost most of my baby weight now, but I spent two years studying how food affects my body while participating in a diverse exercise regimen. I lost weight when living healthily became my lifelong motivator instead of a quick-fix scam.

It's hard to choose "healthy" over "hurry" in our physical life, but it's also difficult in our spiritual life. It's hard to trust Jesus with the timeline of your dream when you're so afraid of missing out—when everybody else has that dream job, adoring husband, perfect kids, financial stability, or

> **JESUS WANTS TO GIVE YOU THE DESIRES OF YOUR HEART . . . WHEN YOU'RE READY.**

platform of influence. It's hard to wait on Jesus when a little work could bring you what you want. Our world teaches that the fulfillment of our dreams will bring us ultimate happiness. But let me ask you a few questions. If chasing your dream steers your hearts away from Jesus, is it worth it? Will you be happy? Would you rather chase an emotional boost or be spiritually healthy? Would you rather Jesus invested in your spiritual health or just gave you an emotional boost?

Jesus wants to give you the desires of your heart . . . when you're ready. He wants you to be happy and healthy. If you have unfulfilled dreams or feel overlooked or undervalued, your sin self might be tempting you with these words, "Don't love Jesus more when he's not giving you what you need!"

Wake up, dear friend. Turn off that sin self's voice and tune in to the truth of your redeemed self. James 1 says, "Consider it pure joy my brothers and sisters whenever you face trials of many kinds, because you know that the testing of your faith produces perseverance. Let perseverance finish its work so that you may be mature and complete, not lacking anything" (James 1:2-4). If your dream seems to be in a holding pattern, if you feel like you're in a trial, then you're not ready for its fulfillment. If we hurry our dreams into existence before we're ready, we won't be healthy or mature enough to handle them. Jesus doesn't keep our dreams at arm's length to torture us, but to keep our hearts healthy. Are you ready to choose health over hurry?

RESET #2: CHRIST OVER CRISIS

For this second motivator reset, we will travel back in time to learn how to choose Christ over our crisis. Imagine you're Peter, Jesus' disciple. You've followed your teacher for three years, watching him perform miracle after miracle. Jesus has just washed your feet and served you the Passover meal. But then, he turns toward you and prophesies, "This very night you will fall away. Truly, I tell you, this very night, before the rooster crows, you will disown me three times" (Matthew 26:31, 34). You try to reassure Jesus of your loyalty with these words, "Even if I have to die with you, I will never disown you" (Matthew 26:35). But Jesus looks at you, and you doubt yourself.

Later, Jesus leads you to the Garden of Gethsemane to pray. You try to stay awake to pray with him, but your eyes can't resist sleep's enticement. Christ carries his burden alone, and you wonder if your sleeping is a betrayal. You wake to a swarm of Roman soldiers entering the garden. They are after Jesus, so there's no time for grogginess. Adrenaline is pumping through your system as you wonder if this is your predicted falling away. Resolute, you draw your sword to defend Jesus and fight against your predicted betrayal. In the chaos, you lose sight of your Savior as you slice off a soldier's ear. You're shocked by your violence, and so is Jesus. He rebukes you, "No more of this!" (Luke 22:51). And he *touches* the man's ear and *heals* him. You were trying so hard not to disappoint Jesus, but instead of appreciation, he rebukes you in front of everyone.

Jesus' rebuke was a reset. Peter was probably so afraid to fail that he lost sight of Christ altogether. If he'd been watching Jesus, he would have seen him surrender. This may have confused Peter, but it would have kept him out of crisis mode, which caused him to cut off a man's ear. When you encounter a confusing or disastrous situation, do you follow Jesus' lead or try to solve the problem yourself? I usually go into panic mode, trying to solve and fix the situation. Choosing Christ over crisis means we stop, take a minute, day, or week to pray, and let go of the tendency to control the situation. We try to see our trial through the lens of joy knowing that our hearts will soon thank us for choosing Christ over crisis.

Peter could have run from Jesus in the garden, but he chose to follow him to the courtyard for Jesus' trial. Jesus didn't defend himself, and Peter's dreams seemed to be dying in front of his eyes. Scared and unsure, Peter entered crisis mode again. Jesus didn't act according to Peter's expectations, and soon after, three crows from a rooster. He's denied his Lord three times. How can Peter come back from such a terrible failure? His dreams fell apart all around him, but Jesus didn't give up on him. Let me show you.

During the Passover meal, when Jesus predicted Peter's denial, he promised to pray for him. He said, "I have prayed for you, Simon, that your faith may not fail. And when you have turned back, strengthen your brothers" (Luke 22:32). I used to believe that Jesus' prayer was intended to prevent Peter's denial. Instead, I think he was praying for Peter's

> EVEN IN HIS LAST MOMENTS ON EARTH, JESUS WAS TRAINING HIS DISCIPLES HOW TO CHOOSE PEACE OVER PANIC, ACTION OVER REACTION, HEALTH OVER HURRY, CHRIST OVER CRISIS, AND SERVICE OVER SELF.

comeback. Jesus was praying that his predetermined forgiveness of Peter before the denial would give him fortitude to forgive himself in retrospect. In Gethsemane, Jesus knew who he was and what he was called to do. He wasn't building an army of soldiers, but of servants. Even in his last moments on earth, Jesus was training his disciples how to choose peace over panic, action over reaction, health over hurry, Christ over crisis, and service over self.

In the garden and at Jesus' trial, Peter was not yet the man the church could depend on, but Jesus used both of their darkest hours to mold him. Jesus didn't give up, and neither did Peter! At the end of his life, Peter chose Christ over crisis when, according to church history, he was crucified upside down. He became exactly who Jesus called him to be, but I'm guessing his life played out a little differently in real life than how Peter dreamed.

> **GOD'S WILL FOR YOUR LIFE IS NOT A SERIES OF PLANNED EXPERIENCES, BUT RATHER A PERSON HE'S DESIGNED YOU TO BECOME.**

If we want to love Jesus more than our dreams, we have to *be* before we *do* and fix our broken motivators by choosing healthy over hurry and Christ over crisis. God's will for your life is not a series of planned experiences, but rather a person he's designed you to become. If you chase your dream more than you chase Jesus, you will be tempted to choose crisis over Christ because the desire for your dream will override the desire to become. This final story will further illustrate this idea.

A DREAM FULFILLED

As I write this book on my iPad, there's a small part of me

doubting these words will ever be published. Right now, I want to type these words to you: "The book you're holding in your hands is a dream fulfilled." But I'm hesitant to believe this dream will come to fruition. Here's why.

I am the queen of put-your-dreams-on-the-back-burner for the sake of your children, your husband's calling, the ministry, whatever "bigger thing" is outweighing my little ol' dream. I've resented God for asking me to make space in my life to help others fulfill their dreams. Watching mine waste away while theirs fall into their laps is torturous. I've felt selfish for wanting what I want but also justified in my selfishness because I've sacrificed so much. I've been mad at Jesus for making me wait, but I've also appreciated the humility he's produced in my soul. Do you see the storm in my soul between my sin self and redeemed self? Have you felt it too?

I wrote my first version of this book in 2003. I sold a thousand copies but didn't republish because it felt incomplete. Finally, in 2012, my brain had the space to create a solid idea for the final product. Since then I have been writing, reworking, and rewriting. I hope to publish this baby in 2017. That's fifteen years of putting my dream on the shelf, of wondering if it would die in me before it became anything at all.

My fifteen years of book resets have been frustrating, but I've learned that health is better than hurry and Christ is better than crisis. Sitting right here, right now, I know my motivator is lined up because I'd be okay if Jesus told me to wait. I'm not going to lie—I'd be disappointed. But I'm more in love with him than my calling to write. Why? Because he is my calling. To know

> IF I'M A CHRIST-FOLLOWER, I HAVE TO LEARN TO CHASE HIM MORE THAN I CHASE MY DREAMS.

him, to become like him, and to make him known to the world is more important than publishing a book. If I'm a Christ-follower, I have to learn to chase him more than I chase my dreams. This is what it means to love him more than our dreams.

CHAPTER 8

I Love You More in My Community

"There's nothing more life giving than giving your life away."
— My friend, Margie Bear

THE GIVING TREE

My boys and I are cuddled on the couch with the book *everyone* says we have to read, *The Giving Tree*. Before I start, I make sure the book is completely centered because reading at their age is all about the pictures. "Okay guys! Everyone says this book is ah-ma-zing, so let's take everyone's word for it and read it today!"

The book begins sweetly. A small boy becomes friends with an apple tree. He is content to be in her presence, sitting in her shade, climbing her limbs, and enjoying her sweet apples. But soon he grows up and needs more from the tree than simple enjoyment. First, he needs money, so the tree happily offers him her apples to sell. The boy disappears for a while but returns later because he needs to build a house. My heart becomes heavy, and my eyes start to water because I know where this is going. I start to cry. My kids look up at me confused, but I compose myself to read this *"great"* book. The tree happily offers him her wood, which the boy is happy to harvest. He leaves again and forgets about the kind tree because she has nothing left to offer but her stump. Now, tears are flowing down my face. I'm not sure my kids are getting the symbolism, but they begin to stroke my arm to comfort me. He doesn't return to see the tree until he is an old man. Perhaps he is all alone in this world, so in his loneliness, he remembers his forgotten friend, now only a stump. When he arrives, the tree apologizes for having nothing left to give the boy, but the old man wants to sit on her stump. And the tree is happy.

"Boys, how did you like that book?" I ask.

"Good" is their unified reaction. The symbolism is completely over their head, and they don't know what to do with their teary-eyed mom . . . so they slide off the couch and start playing.

But I just sit. I'm mesmerized by the sketch drawing of the boy taking one apple from the happy tree. My kids play and scream behind me, but I'm deep in thought. I am convicted. The boy feels like me. I feel like a taker in my friendships. I don't want to be, but deep down, I know I'm more like the boy than the tree. I want to be the happy giving tree, but I know I'm not. As I sit, my sin self speaks to me, "The tree is the fool, not the boy. What person in their right mind would give everything to a selfish boy who doesn't appreciate the gift or the giver? Getting is gaining. Giving is a risk that will come back to haunt you."

When I travel and speak, friendship is always a hot topic. I've noticed we are struggling to do friendships well. We are afraid to give too much. We are afraid someone will take advantage of us, talk about us behind our backs, share our deepest, darkest secrets, bully us. Or perhaps we're afraid to love someone who might later trade our friendship in for a newer, fresher model. Are you a little bit afraid of friendships? I know it's scary, but if we want to love Jesus better in our friendships, we have to start trying. We have to believe giving, not getting, is gaining.

GIVING IS GAINING

When I was a schoolgirl, I remember thinking, "If *those people* liked me I'd be popular, important, find a boyfriend, and fit in." The combination of a social life at school and entertainment on the weekends taught me that friendships existed to meet my emotional needs or make me popular. I thought an ideal friend would always listen and never disagree because I dreaded conflict. She would share all of my likes and none of my dislikes because then we'd always love hanging out. She would always lift me up and never drain me because then I'd always go home happy.

She would always be there for me, but never inconvenience me. A friend like this may seem perfect *in theory*, but realistically, she would've turned me into a selfish mess. This is why getting isn't gaining; it's detrimental to our overall wellbeing and spiritual growth. God doesn't give us friends to satisfy all our desires, but to help us run our race and finish life well. "Getting is gaining" may be the message the world teaches, but *giving is gaining* is the message of our Savior.

Scripture says, "Greater love has no one than this: to lay down one's life for one's friends" (John 15:13). The message of *The Giving Tree* is similar to the gospel. The tree was happy to give her life to the boy just as Jesus joyfully gave

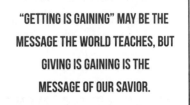

> "GETTING IS GAINING" MAY BE THE MESSAGE THE WORLD TEACHES, BUT GIVING IS GAINING IS THE MESSAGE OF OUR SAVIOR.

every ounce of his breath, his blood, and his life for our freedom. When we love Jesus more in our friendships, we show our love for one another by laying our lives down, not using others to make our lives better.

This is easier said than done. It's easier to invest in love that has a good return. Love that costs too much feels unsafe and risky. But if our goal is to love Jesus more in our friendships, we need to become *used to* laying our lives down for one another. When we give ourselves to one another we all grow and become strong together instead of becoming apathetic and lazy.

THE COFFEE SHOP

She had a captive audience. We'd listened to her stories in the coffee shop for over an hour, but it felt like twenty minutes. She had that super-funny-hard-to-resist personality. She was a true entertainer—a master storyteller who knew what accents, facial expressions, and dramatic pauses to use at just the right times. Maybe she had a second job as a stand-up comedian. She wore confidence like it was her favorite outfit, and her people skills were unmatched by anyone I knew (except maybe my husband). But then, as we walked out to our cars, she confessed, "I'm not good at friendships." I was shocked. How could someone with so much likability feel insecure in her friendships?

Initially, I was confused by her statement until the Lord showed me that she was me a few years ago. You see, when Clayton and I were first married, we traveled extensively—meeting new people in new places every week. People wanted to know how we met and where we'd been, and we were happy to share because they left satisfied. We became used to entertaining, and soon, our conversations felt scripted like a play.

Years later, I drove home from having coffee with a friend. My hands gripped the steering wheel as I stared into the setting sun and processed our time together. Each word, every sentence, rolled around in my mind. As I dissected the good and the bad, I was horrified to realize that most of the conversation had been about me: my concerns, my hurts, my frustrations, and my dreams. Didn't she say *anything*? Oh yes, she did, but to my detriment, I couldn't even remember *what* because when she spoke I was too busy trying to find my response. I am definitely exaggerating a little bit, but I had a revelation that day. I thought the conversational skills I'd learned on the road with strangers would easily translate into my friendships, but they didn't. If my tear-stained pillow could talk to you, it would share that I was surrounded by people, but felt alone. I wanted to be close, to feel close to my friends, but I didn't know how to open up. I didn't know how to engage someone else in conversation because I was too busy entertaining. If I wanted to love Jesus more in my friendships, I needed to put myself on the shelf. I needed to stop feeling the pressure of carrying the conversation and just start listening.

PUT YOURSELF ON THE SHELF

There's nothing wrong with telling entertaining stories or developing good conversational skills. But if we want to take our friendships deeper, we have to do away with conversational monologues. Friends want a two-way conversation with you; they don't want to be talked *at*, but *to*. Are you any different? You want people to listen and try to understand you, right?

I was cooking dinner while my kids were watching a teenage melodrama. Since I was busy, I wasn't watching the show, only listening. Have you ever noticed that every conversation in a teenage melodrama is a monologue? Parents, kids, teenagers, and teachers each talk *at* each other *about themselves*. Very rarely do they interact with one another in a conversation. Instead, the dialogue is full of introspective speeches followed by scripted sarcastic quips and whining. They don't take time to pause or listen to one another because they're too busy formulating comebacks.

We know teenage melodramas aren't real, but I wonder if we do our conversations much differently. Are we good at pausing, looking at one another in the eye, and listening? Have we lost the skill of caring conversation because we're so self-consumed?

We don't have to become expert conversationalists, but we do need Jesus to teach us how to put ourselves on the shelf. We need him to teach us the lost art of loving by laying our lives down for one another. Your sin self doesn't want you to lay your life down. It will use your vanity to lie to you. Your vanity will convince you that you need to shine brighter so other people will like you more. But no one is attracted to an elevated human ego. Vanity will try to fill your void with self-focus. But genuine value is only found from a focus turned vertical. We cannot love our friends deeply if we're not willing to love them more than ourselves. We will not find a friend who loves us deeply if we're not willing to put ourselves on the shelf. We have to sacrifice our need to shine brighter and turn the light on our friend instead.

Let me show you what this looks like in real life. When I realized that my conversations were self-focused, I asked the Lord to help me put myself on the shelf, and he showed me this verse, "Give, and it will be given to you. A good measure, pressed down, shaken together, and running over, will be poured into your lap. For with the measure you use, it will be measured back to you" (Luke 6:38). I asked myself how I could be more giving in my coffee conversations. My solution was simple. Ask them the same questions I'd want to be asked:

- How are you doing?
- What's going on in your life?
- What's your biggest dream?
- Is there anything I could do to be a better friend?

So I tried it. At first, I struggled to focus, listen, and not interrupt my friend with my own comments or solutions. Their words kept triggering thoughts, ideas, memories, and stories I wanted to share, but I kept my mouth shut and my responses short. I felt like my dog, Niko, when I place a treat right in front of his nose but don't let him have it. He gets anxious and jittery. His tail wags and eyes dart, and his breath becomes labored. The self-control felt excruciating. But I did it.

I practiced keeping quiet over and over, and as I did, I felt myself melting into each friend's life story. I empathized with their struggles and felt joy in their accomplishments. I enjoyed being on the shelf and letting them shine because I realized they were trusting me with their treasures. My silent attention welcomed an intimacy I hadn't known; it was a treat worth the self-control. I learned to give, and a deeper love and affection was given to me in a measure that was "pressed down, shaken together, and running over."

RUTH AND NAOMI

One time, on an international bus ride, I was playing a question game with friends to pass the time. The question we had to answer was, "If you could be any person in the Bible, who would you choose?" When my friend answered Ruth, the reality of living Ruth's life hit me like a ton of bricks.

Ruth and her mother-in-law, Naomi, had lost everything: spouses, children, and belongings. With nothing to keep Naomi in Moab, she decided to return home to her own people, the Jews, whom she had abandoned previously because there was a famine. Since Naomi had nothing to offer Ruth, and since the Jews weren't fond of Ruth's nationality, Naomi encouraged her to stay in Moab, but Ruth refused.

Ruth put herself on the shelf to serve her mother-in-law. Ruth's loyal love earned her the company of a bitter and hopeless mother-in-law. Not only was Naomi unpleasant, but the Jews shunned the two women when they first arrived in the new land. Ruth spent her days begging for grain in the hot sun, but she continued to love Naomi. If you've read the story, you know that Ruth's devotion to her mother-in-law eventually paid off. Her hard work and loyalty caught the attention of a godly man who asked her to be his wife. Ruth and Boaz were the great-grandparents of King David and part of the lineage of Jesus.

When Ruth left her home with Naomi, she didn't know that putting herself on the shelf would bring her such a legacy. When she was laboring under the scorching sun, begging for her next meal, she didn't know that Boaz would rescue and marry her. She simply loved Naomi like Jesus loved us. And while Ruth appreciated the physical benefits of a husband, home, and influential position in society, I wonder if her mother's escape from the claws of bitterness was a more precious gift. Ruth is a biblical picture of *The Giving Tree*. She found joy in giving herself so that Naomi could gain.

Ruth took a risk that paid off, but I wonder what fears she had to overcome to put herself on the shelf.

- Would her loneliness would increase?
- Would she run out of love or energy?
- Would Naomi ever appreciate her sacrifice?

- Will there be a payoff? Should she even want or expect that?

Ruth put herself on the shelf and found victory over her fears. One of the human heart's greatest needs is to feel loved, valued, and accepted, so putting ourselves on the shelf feels like a risk. Our sin self tells us to fill our void with the love of people around us. But what if the people we're loving can't reciprocate our love? What if God calls us to love a Naomi?

> IF WE WANT TO LOVE OUR FRIENDS MORE THAN WE LOVE OURSELVES, WE HAVE TO LET JESUS FILL OUR LOVE VOID.

If we want to love our friends more than we love ourselves, we have to let Jesus fill our love void. We have to transition where we seek affection! We start to love each other more when we believe that giving is gaining, when we decide putting ourselves on the shelf is worth it, and finally, when we choose to believe the best about one another.

MR. BOO FAN

My family is sitting second row for a Clemson home game. I knew it was going to be noisy. I expected it. But, there's a man behind us who knows *everything* and won't stop yelling into the back of my head. Part of me wishes he'd just put on a jersey and show us all how the game should be played. And just when I don't think he can get any more obnoxious—he does. The refs make a few bad calls against our beloved team, and he loses it! *"What's wrong with you, ref?"* Then—at the top of his lungs—he yells a long-winded *"Boooo!"* at every play for the rest of the game. I agree with his assessment, but I'm more irritated with Mr. Boo Fan than the refs because he's keeping me from appreciating my second-row seats!

When the opposing team sustains their fourth injury, I can't take it anymore. I sit on my seat covering my ears while Mr. Boo Fan shouts out his conspiracy theories, "Y'all ain't injured. You're just trying to ruin our momentum! Your guy is faking it." A medical team surrounds the player, so we can't tell what's going on, but Mr. Boo Fan shouts his prophecies, "He isn't hurt! I bet this guy hops up and gets right back in the game." I feel Mr. Boo Fan's skepticism creeping into my emotions. I'm starting to believe his conspiracy when the injured player rises from the middle of the crowd wearing a black and red cast on his arm. A golf cart pulls up to carry him away, and under his breath Mr. Boo Fan confesses, "Well, I guess he is hurt." Then he screams at their bench, "My bad!" My frustration with him releases as he confesses his error.

BELIEVING THE BEST

I wonder how many times I have been *Mrs.* Boo Fan in my

friendships. I wonder how many times I've misinterpreted a friend's words or actions. I wonder how many times I was too scared or prideful to try to understand, listen, or work things out. I wonder how much time I've spent analyzing what "she" said—what she meant, what I think she was going to say, or even worse, what she meant by what she was going to say. I wonder how many times I had *her* figured out and thought I knew *everything* . . . until I discovered I knew nothing at all.

A few years ago, I attended a leadership conference where Andy Stanley preached. One of his quotes changed my perspective in my friendships. He said, "The one thing successful relationships all have in common is the inclination to immediately *believe the best* about their friend or significant other in the midst of failure or miscommunication." As I listened to him, I realized that I wanted a friend who would understand, forgive, and give me the benefit of the doubt. I wanted a friend who wouldn't judge me, but who would believe the best. I wanted a friend who wouldn't jump to a rash conclusion about my character based on a moment of weakness.

But I also wondered how often I'm this kind of friend to others. How often do I believe the best?

We all fail our friends. We say things we don't mean. We're habitually inconsiderate, rude, and easily offended. We withdraw and give up when we should pursue and work through a problem. We don't intend to hurt one another, but we're imperfectly human. God is our only perfect friend. With this in mind, we have to let go of the preposterous assumption that anyone will love us as well as Jesus does. In friendship, conflict and disappointment are inevitable. If we want friendships that last, we have to free each other from the shackles of perfect performance and believe the best about each other. I wonder how many friendships we could save if we chose to believe the best.

It's hard to believe the best about someone who has failed us. When I got in trouble as a little girl, my mom, grandmother, teachers, and everyone

> **WE HAVE TO LET GO OF THE PREPOSTEROUS ASSUMPTION THAT ANYONE WILL LOVE US AS WELL AS JESUS DOES.**

would say, "Do to others as you would have them do to you" (Luke 6:31). I'd roll my eyes, cross my arms, and exhale frustrated. I *dreaded* those words because even though they felt right, I just didn't want to *do* them! But people will not believe the best about us if we're not choosing to believe the best about them. The greater you give, the deeper you receive. When you believe the best about someone else, it keeps your heart clear of bitterness and gives them permission to believe the best about you.

Ecclesiastes 4:9 says, "Two are better than one because they have a good return for their work. If one falls down, his friend can help him up . . . a cord of three strands is not quickly broken" (Ecclesiastes 4:9, 12b). Life isn't easy, and I know friendships aren't either. But God has given us each other to encourage and build each other up, help each other run our race of faith, and give each other strength when we're down. If we truly believe that two are better than one and a cord of three strands is harder to break, we have to buy into the idea that giving, not getting, is gaining. We must be willing to put ourselves on the shelf

> WHEN YOU BELIEVE THE BEST ABOUT SOMEONE ELSE, IT KEEPS YOUR HEART CLEAR OF BITTERNESS AND GIVES THEM PERMISSION TO BELIEVE THE BEST ABOUT YOU.

and believe the best about one another. When we love Jesus more in our friendships, we start serving others instead of ourselves and soon come to understand that investing in the lives of others brings joy and satisfaction to our own souls. God has called us to be light and salt in this world. He has called us to do friendships differently. We won't be perfect, but we can sure try and watch him work miracles in our lives and the lives of those we love!

CHAPTER 9

I Love You More with My Future

---

*"Sometimes you just need twenty seconds
of insane courage."*
— Benjamin Mee, *We Bought a Zoo*

CRAZY RISK

I open an email from a friend: "Do you want to go sky-diving?" My husband has bragged about all the times he's been, so I competitively put it on my bucket list. But now that the opportunity is staring me in the face, I'm having second thoughts. I *can* reply, "No," but I don't. A few months later, I pull into the flight school parking lot with my family. I *can* turn around, but I don't. As I sign my life away, gear up, and wait on a bench to board the plane, I *can* leave, but I don't. The flight school boards the plane, and as it climbs in altitude, I stare out the window. Technically, I *can* still abort this mission, but I don't. It's time to jump, so my instructor taps my shoulder, smiles, and gives me the thumbs-up sign. I am *not* smiling, but as he stands, I do too because I have no choice; he's strapped to my back. I want to run to the rear of the plane and curl up in the fetal position, but his confidence guides me forward. I assume he wants to live, so he will keep me alive for the sake of his own survival. My feet are planted on the edge of the open door, and my hands are clenching the metal bar above my head. The sky is daring me to jump, but my hands won't let go, so the instructor gives me the thumbs-up again. As I mindlessly let go of the bar to reciprocate, he gives me a sneaky grin and swings us into the open air.

I try to scream, but I can't breathe. The air is speeding past my mouth too fast to inhale. I had anticipated that I might die from a faulty parachute, but certainly not from suffocation. As I try to figure out if I'm dying or not, my instructor has the audacity to yell, *"Are you okay?"* I don't answer because I can't breathe. Besides, he wouldn't be able to hear me say, "No! I'm suffocating, you fool!" I suppose he'll figure out I'm dead when we hit the ground. Seconds later, he pulls the shoot. My body jerks up, and instead of falling at an unimaginable speed, we start to float. The parachute worked, and now I can breathe! All I have to fear now is the landing.

We float in a wide circular pattern that keeps getting smaller as we approach the runway. I'm starting to enjoy myself when my instructor says, "Get ready to jog in the landing." Jog in what? I can't feel my legs. I don't remember jogging or the landing, but I do remember my husband and two boys running and tackling me with hugs when I reached the ground. As we drive away from the skydiving school, I think to myself, "That was a risk. A crazy risk. I'm glad that's off my bucket list, and I'm even more glad I didn't pee on myself in the process."

When my son, Joseph, played goalie for his soccer team, he risked being trampled every time he dove after the ball. I asked him once how he mentally handled the fear, and he wisely replied, "You know Mama, sometimes you just have to do crazy things. You don't know how they're going to turn out, but you take the risk anyway."

We take crazy risks every day—driving a car, flying in a plane, walking beside a busy road, birthing a baby, falling in love, forgiving an offense, committing to marriage, pursuing a dream, or buying a house. It's easier to take a risk when we're given the chance to weigh out the consequences. But how do we trust Jesus with our future when it feels like he's asking us to jump out of a perfectly safe plane? How do we jump when he says, "Jump"?

MOSES

Moses was born to be a rescuer—it was the meaning of his name. Rescuing was in his nature. When he was a baby, his mom refused to obey Pharaoh's edict to kill her baby. Instead, she packed him in a basket and sent him down the river. He was discovered by Pharaoh's daughter who raised him to read, write, and command competently. When Moses discovered that his ethnicity was Hebrew instead of Egyptian, his rescuer heart broke as he witnessed an Egyptian taskmaster beating a Hebrew slave. Infuriated, Moses rescued the Hebrew but killed the slave driver in the process. This disastrous rescue attempt turned Pharaoh against him, so Moses fled to the desert, found a wife, and joined her father's family business of shepherding. One day, Moses was taking care of the sheep when he became distracted by a bush that seemed to be burning, but refused to be consumed. Curiosity lured Moses closer. God used the bush to capture Moses' attention and then invited him to take a crazy risk.

When my kids were little, I used to play hide-and-seek with them. I tried to hide in an easy-to-find place, but more often than not, I'd hide too well for their searching eyes. I would have to make noises to give away my hiding place, and if that didn't work, I'd call out their name. If *this* didn't work, I'd crawl to find them and act super surprised when they bumped into me. God lured Moses to himself by hiding in a bush.

When Adam and Eve were afraid of God, they hid in a bush because they were afraid. Perhaps God hid because he wanted Moses to search and find him. Perhaps God appeared in a bush, rather than as an angelic presence, because he hoped to disarm Moses' fear. Since the first time Moses tried to rescue a Hebrew slave on his own he murdered a man, Moses probably feared that God would soon come to judge him. God's presence in the bush was a disarming invitation to redeem Moses' most shameful moment. God invited Moses to help him rescue an entire nation.

"Moses," God says, "I have indeed seen the misery of my people in Egypt. I have heard them crying because of their slave drivers, and I am concerned about those suffering. So I have come down to rescue them from the hand of the Egyptians and to bring them up out of that land into a good and spacious land. So now, go. I am sending you to Pharaoh to bring my people the Israelites up out of Egypt" (Exodus 3:7-10). What was Moses' response? "Yes Lord! I've heard their cries too and have been waiting for you to call me to come to their aid!" Nope. Moses was afraid to take the crazy risk.

DO NOT BE AFRAID

Have you ever thought, "If I knew then what I know now, I would have done things differently"? Life is full of lessons, so hindsight is often 20/20. Standing in front of the bush that day, Moses wasn't fond of the path God was asking him to take. So, let's travel forward in Moses' life to the moment he parts the Red Sea. How did he conquer his fear in that moment, and how can we apply it to his future?

Egypt has suffered many infuriating plagues, and finally, Pharaoh is fed up enough to order the Hebrew exodus. God's rescue plan seems to finally be working until the Israelites see Pharaoh and his soldiers behind them in hot pursuit. The Egyptian army finds the Israelites on the border of the Red Sea. The Hebrews are afraid to die by the sword, so they lash out at Moses. "Didn't we say to you in Egypt, 'Leave us alone; let us serve the Egyptians'? It would have been better for us to serve the Egyptians than to die in the desert" (Exodus 14:12). The Israelites' freedom is blocked by an immovable ocean when Moses offers this word of faith, "Do not be afraid. Stand firm and you will see the deliverance the Lord will bring to you today. The Egyptians you see today you will never see again. The LORD will fight for you; you need only be still" (Exodus 14:13-14). After encouraging the Israelites, Moses' own faith falters for a quick minute, but then the Lord says to Moses:

> "Why are you crying out to me? Tell the Israelites to move on. Raise your staff and stretch out your hand over the sea to divide the water so that the Israelites can go through the sea on dry ground . . ." Then Moses stretched out his hand over the sea, and that night the Lord drove the sea back with a strong east wind and turned

it into dry land. The waters were divided, and the Israelites went through the sea on dry ground, with a wall of water on their right and on their left. (Exodus 14:15-16, 21-22)

God's vision is never impaired because his sight is always 20/20. But our faith is hindered by previous experiences, misperceptions, insecurities, and bad advice. If future Moses were to offer himself hindsight advice at the burning bush, what would he have told himself? "Do not be afraid. Stand firm and you will see the deliverance the Lord will bring . . . The LORD will fight for you; you need only be still" (Exodus 14:13-14).

God's calling can feel scary, confusing, and intimidating. But he pursues each of us in a way we will understand. He wrestled with Jacob, worshiped with the shepherds, spoke to Elijah in a wind, led the magi with a star, and hid in a bush for Moses. His calling for you

> WE LOVE HIM MORE BY CHOOSING NOT TO BE AFRAID, STANDING FIRM, AND WATCHING AS HE DELIVERS US.

will be unique to your gifts and personality. He won't ask you to do something out of character, and he won't push you out of the nest before you're ready to fly. However, when you jump out, the first few flaps might certainly be frightening. If we want to love him more with our future, we have to walk over to that open door, let go as he swings us out, and trust that he will guide us to our destiny. We love him more by choosing not to be afraid, standing firm, and watching as he delivers us.

STAND FIRM

A friend of mine watched a video of a Brené Brown conference where Brene was speaking to a crowd of counselors. She asked them all to stand and act out their coolest dance and sport their coolest stance. She perused the crowd from one side to the other and then asked the crowd what sort of vibe their posture might be sending her way. A few spoke up: untouchable, angry, cool, unapproachable, and intimidating. This was her point: the way American culture projects cool is not at all attractive in an actual person. We don't want to be stand-offish, cold-hearted, or unapproachable. How ironic that so many would subconsciously strike that kind of pose in an attempt to project "cool."

When I say the words "stand firm," what picture comes to your mind? Possibly an old-school armor-plated army ready for battle with tough faces and steel swords. My mind imagines a *Lord of the Rings*, or *Braveheart* stand-off battle. And since we're talking about movies, when the camera zooms in on a battle scene, what does it capture? A doubtful face here and a scared face there. A boy who seems too young to fight but is on the battle lines anyway. The face I remember the most from a battle scene is a woman from *Lord of the Rings*. Eowyn hides herself in men's battle gear and mounts her horse to fight the demons of Mordor. She stands, not because she is brave, but because she wants to fight for her kingdom's future. She is terrified, but she sends her doubt packing to fulfill a calling. I want to be this woman, don't you? What is Jesus calling you to be?

When God invited Moses to join his rescue mission, he had five excuses. These excuses can keep us from loving Jesus more with our future, so we're going to rip the roots out of them and plant seeds of faith in their place. Let's send our excuses packing.

1. DON'T QUIT WHEN YOU THINK GOD SHOULD PICK SOMEONE ELSE.

Moses was afraid he wasn't the right man for the job. When God asked him to rescue the Israelites, his first response was, "Who am I?" Moses was raised in a palace with the knowledge to command an army, so it seems like he had the skills to fit the bill, but his previous rescue attempt turned him into a murderer. He was afraid of trying another one.

As the son of Pharaoh, Moses was taught to place confidence in his abilities and power, but now God was teaching Moses to become a different kind of general. God assured Moses, "I will be with you." When Moses didn't feel like the right man for the job, God promised to be with him and lead him.

Sometimes we're afraid to love God more with our future because we're intimidated. When we experience insecurity, we have to rest in God's identity. It's not about who we are, but who God is. Our obedience initiates his work in our lives. You might be afraid or feel like someone else could do the job better, but God is choosing you. His invitation came to *your* inbox, not someone else's. Will you obey?

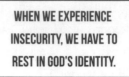

WHEN WE EXPERIENCE INSECURITY, WE HAVE TO REST IN GOD'S IDENTITY.

2. DON'T QUIT WHEN PEOPLE DON'T TRUST YOU.

Moses was afraid to become Israel's deliverer because he was an outsider. Would they believe God sent him? He wondered how the Israelites would respond to an outsider prancing into their camp, announcing, "The God of your fathers sent me to be your deliverer!" Would they receive him, or would they interrogate him? "Who are you to lead us? We don't even know you. Didn't you grow up in the palace as one of Pharaoh's sons? Your 'family' has enslaved us for generations. Why should we trust you?"

When you're trying to love Jesus more with your future, you have to trust God as your general. When you don't have a position, rest in his commission. When people don't trust me, I worry about how I am going to prove myself to them. This is wasted energy. If someone has withdrawn their trust, no amount of explanation or arguing will change their mind. Don't let doubters distract you from God's calling. God is your general, so settle yourself under his authority and set your hands to the plow. Hopefully, as you "let your light shine before others, *they will see* your good deeds and glorify your Father in heaven" (Matthew 5:16, emphasis mine).

3. DON'T QUIT WHEN PEOPLE DON'T BELIEVE IN YOUR CALLING.

Moses was afraid the people would not believe he was called by God. Perhaps Moses didn't know how to explain a calling he hadn't quite accepted or didn't quite understand. How do we prove we're called when people (or maybe we) don't see what God sees? When we don't have proof, we have to rest in

> **WHEN WE DON'T HAVE PROOF, WE HAVE TO REST IN HIS PROVISION.**

his provision. God gave Moses a few tools to boost his confidence: a snake-staff, a miraculous healing-hand, and the ability to turn water into blood. But I'm sure he still wondered if those tools would work when he tried them out in Pharaoh's palace. What if Pharaoh didn't believe in Moses' calling? What if Pharaoh didn't listen to him or refused to release God's people from his grips? What if Moses couldn't make his calling work?

When we don't have concrete proof of what God has called us to, we have to believe in his provision. When God says, "Let's go," our job is to stand with him, follow him to that open sky, and let him launch us out of the plane, knowing that he packed the parachute correctly, knows when to release it, and will competently jog us in for the landing. "The one who calls you is faithful, and he will do it" (1 Thessalonians 5:24). So jump. Your obedience will initiate God's work.

4. DON'T QUIT WHEN PEOPLE SEE YOUR DEFICIENCIES.

Moses is afraid because God is asking him to give a speech to the most powerful man in the region, and Moses stutters. He doesn't want to broadcast his weakness to the world, so he responds, "O Lord, I have never been eloquent, neither in the past, nor since you have spoken to your servant. I am slow of speech and tongue" (Exodus 4:10).

Have you ever felt broken? You are too shy, too opinionated, too easily offended, too passive, too . . . you get the picture. I understand feeling incapable, but Moses' words make me giggle a little. He informs his Maker that not only has he not spoken well in the past, *but his speech hasn't improved while they have been conversing.* In other words, "God, you've given me a magic staff, a leprosy trick, and the ability to turn water into blood, but why haven't you magically made me a better orator during this conversation?" Moses' comment feels a little sassy to me. He's been trying to talk God out of this calling. "I'm not the right person, I'm not an insider, I don't have authority to make this happen . . ." And now, "I've never been good at speeches, and that hasn't changed, so I'm out."

The first time I taught in front of a large group of people, my leg wouldn't stop shaking, and my voice wouldn't stop quivering. I said too much too fast, and yet the Holy Spirit used that message in spite of my deficiency. God has been teaching me more and more that it's not about who I am, but who he is. I am only capable because God is capable, not the other way around. If we want to love Jesus more with our future, we have to rest in his identity, his calling, and his capability.

> I AM ONLY CAPABLE BECAUSE GOD IS CAPABLE, NOT THE OTHER WAY AROUND.

5. DON'T QUIT WHEN YOU'RE JUST TOO SCARED.

Moses is just plain afraid. He's given God a list of tangible reasons he doesn't want to take the crazy risk, but God isn't listening. So finally, Moses confesses the real reason. He doesn't want to go. He likes his new life in the desert, and he doesn't want to return to the life he left behind.

But God is on a mission to free his people, so he has already paved the way. Moses is standing at the edge of the airplane door, clenching that metal bar, when God gives him the courage to leap out.

> What about your brother, Aaron the Levite? I know he can speak well. He is already on his way to meet you, and he will be glad to see you. You shall speak to him and put words in his mouth; I will help both of you

to speak, and I will teach you what to do. He will speak to the people for you, and it will be as if he were your mouth and you were God to him. But take this staff in your hand so you can perform miraculous signs with it." (Exodus 4:14-17)

This encouragement is God's thumbs-up. Moses is looking out of the plane, terrified, when God points out of the plane toward his brother Aaron who has jumped and is waiting. "Go, Moses! You and Aaron can do this together." Moses was scared to take on the task alone, so God sends Aaron as a support system. I wonder how long it had been since Moses had seen Aaron's face or hugged his neck? The opportunity to fulfill this calling with his brother gave Moses the courage he needed to jump out of the plane. When you want to quit loving Jesus more with your future, ask a friend to walk beside you.

MOVE YOUR MOUNTAIN

It's 1999, and Clayton and I are on a medical mission trip in the Himalayas. We're backpacking 200 miles on foot. We wake up in a tent every morning, grab a quick breakfast, and then pack up for a full day of hiking. Every day we climb these majestic mountains. I know it's the opportunity of a lifetime, but it's not easy. The store we bought our gear from gave me a free quick-dry shirt that says, "The joy is in the journey." Each morning I pull the stinking shirt over my head and argue with it. The joy is *not* in the journey—I should know. I'm the person hiking these peaks, not the ignorant person who branded the ridiculous slogan!

We hike through a valley that opens up to a peak with an elevation of 18,600 feet. Surely we're hiking around this one? Nope. Our guide points toward Mr. Super-High Peak and says, "That's the trail." My mind and body don't believe I will feel joy in this journey—lugging my sore feet, tight neck, aching shoulders, and breathless lungs up *that* mountain. But since there aren't any buses, taxis, or even a road in this area, my feet are responsible for my journey. At least the slanderous slogan is on the back of my shirt covered by my pack.

There are no power outlets built into the Himalayas, so my mind is my entertainment. As I hike, my body rhythm creates the music in my mind . . . a trekking song if you will: *breath, step, step, step, breath, step, step, step.* In the valleys, I have energy for conversation or possibly singing, but the higher altitudes require more air per step. As I ascend, my song changes to: *breath, step, breath, step.* And a little higher: *breath, breath, step.* I'm so tired my mind feels fuzzy, and my eyes blur. I want God to move this mountain, but I'd settle for him moving me to the top if moving the mountain is too disruptive.

I hike, step by step, and breath by breath, until the moment I've been waiting for arrives. The flags on the summit come into view, which means I'm close. They become my goal. My mind is singing *breath, breath, step, breath, breath, step* when I reach the summit. I plop my pack on the ground, dance as best I can in my hiking boots, and scream at the top of my lungs. I made it! With my backpack on the ground, I see the message on my shirt, and I argue with it again, "Stupid shirt—the joy is not in the journey." I wasn't screaming and dancing up that mountain, but I'm dancing now!

I stop a minute (or ten) to stare down the path I just trekked. *I did that!* And then I have this thought: *I conquered that mountain, and the pleasure I'm experiencing is a result of the journey. Eliminate journey, and you take away the celebration.*

I bet Moses didn't see any joy in the journey before him. He felt insufficient, insecure, broken, and deficient. But Moses hiked the mountain anyway. If you read the rest of his story, you'll discover that Moses was abused and used by Pharaoh, rejected and accused by the Israelites, and sometimes felt abandoned by God. Still, Moses and Aaron obeyed God. Each time his journey became increasingly difficult, he chose not to be afraid, stood firm, and watched the Lord use him to deliver the Israelites.

God can move any mountain. God can take away our struggles and make our lives easier. He can move our mountains,

> **GOD CAN CHANGE YOUR SITUATION, OR HE CAN INVITE YOU TO CHANGE SO THAT YOU'RE STRONGER THAN THE SITUATION YOU FACE.**

I've discovered, but more often than not, the mountain he wants to move is *us*. God can change your situation, or he can invite *you* to change so that you're stronger than the situation you face. Moses was a born rescuer. Living in Pharaoh's palace taught him that his rescue was in his own strength, but that ended in regret. A few years as a desert shepherd humbled Moses. He was still a rescuer, but his confidence transferred from his own capability to the Lord's. The Lord moved the mountain of pride out of his soul and built up his faith through a mission of redemption. God wants to teach you how to move the mountains inside you.

There was a season I wanted to quit ministry. I remember telling my husband, "I don't have to stand in front of people, speaking from a heart of vulnerability. I don't have to be a target. I could give it all up for a normal life." But Clayton looked me straight in the eyes and said, "But, Sharie, isn't this your calling?" He was right, but I had a mountain of pain and doubt in my heart. If I was going to love Jesus more with my future, I was going to have to move it. When I was hiking in the Himalayas, I prayed that God would move that mountain out of my way. When that didn't work, I started climbing. At the summit, I gazed down at the path I'd climbed and realized that even though God didn't move the mountain, it was still behind me. He didn't lift it out of the way, but he gave me the strength to summit. My mountain moved because I was willing to climb.

SEE THE DELIVERANCE

Before Moses started his journey, God said, "When you have brought the people out of Egypt, you will worship God on this mountain" (Exodus 3:12). But Moses did not return to the mountain to worship until after the plagues, the Red Sea parting, the wandering, and the complaining. The confirmation of Moses' calling didn't come until the hard labor was completed. When Moses stood on the summit of Mt. Sinai, I wonder if

> I WONDER HOW MANY MIRACLES I'VE MISSED BECAUSE I WAS TOO AFRAID TO MOVE, TOO FOCUSED ON MYSELF, OR JUST QUIT BECAUSE MY CALLING PROVED TOO TOUGH.

he looked down at the people and thought, "God moved mountains, but the biggest mountain was me. I didn't think I was the man for the job, but I'm glad I didn't reject God's calling on my life."

Moses could have remained comfortable in Midian. He could have played it safe, not loving God more with his future. But think about the miracles he would have missed. Wouldn't he have regretted not loving God more with his future?

I wonder how many miracles I've missed because I was too afraid to move, too focused on myself, or just *quit* because my calling proved too tough. I respect Moses for loving God more with his future. We're still benefiting from his obedience. I wonder how many lives his story has impacted.

When you have the chance to quit, when things get too hard, don't play it safe and take the easy route. Don't wait for your mountain to magically move. Keep moving forward. Put one foot of faith in front of the other. You'll climb that mountain and realize that the mountain you needed to move was you!

I wonder how many lives your story will impact when you love Jesus more with your future.

CONCLUSION

Some of the sweetest Jesus moments I've had with my children have come in those wonderful minutes before bedtime. When they were infants I used to sing, "Jesus Loves Me" as I rocked them to sleep. Did you ever sing this simple childhood song?

> Jesus loves me, this I know,
> For the Bible tells me so,
> Little ones to him belong,
> They are weak, but he is strong.
> Yes, Jesus loves me.

To be honest, I sort of felt silly singing it as an adult, but as I did, I remember wishing that my theology was still so simple. I am little and weak, but he is strong. He loves me, so I'm all good. In Mark, a crowd of people brought their children to Jesus because they wanted him to touch them and bless them. Perhaps their kids were sick. They might have wanted Jesus to impart a spiritual blessing to them. Or maybe they were already believers and desperately wanted their little ones to know Jesus too. The disciples tried to send them away, but "when Jesus saw this, he was indignant. He said to them, 'Let the little children come to me, and do not hinder them, for the kingdom of heaven belongs to such as these. Truly I tell you, anyone who will not receive the kingdom of God like a little child will never enter it.' And he took the children in his arms and placed his hands on them and blessed them" (Mark 10:14).

Loving Jesus more is simple . . . if we don't complicate it. We all have different reasons we've let the worries of this world suffocate our childlike faith. I've written this book hoping that my vulnerable honesty will help you uncover some worries that have kept you from experiencing his simple love. We've learned that loving Jesus more is not about working harder, but resting in the work he's already accomplished on the cross. It's not about keeping ourselves from pain, but knowing he's with us and will heal us when we hurt. It's not about earning his favor, but knowing he loved us before he placed us in our mother's womb. It's not about earning his favor, but crawling up into his lap and letting him wrap his arms around us and bless us.

When my kids were babies, I was afraid they would become tired of Jesus and church considering so much of their existence was spent around my husband and me serving people in ministry. And then, one day, I had a revelation. *Jesus loves my kids more than I do.* I had to learn to trust Jesus more than I trusted myself with my kids.

The other night, I came home from writing this very book. When I opened the door from the garage into the house, a light from Jacob's room was shining under his door. It was super late, and past his bedtime, so I was ready to institute some parental discipline. I knocked on his door, and he said, "Come in." My mood changed instantly when I opened the door and found him on his knees beside his bed, praying. I couldn't believe that my fourteen-year-old teenager was on his knees before his Lord! My heart was so glad.

"Hey, buddy. I was just checking on you. I hope you have a good prayer time, but you need to get some sleep baby, okay?"

I don't know how Jesus did it, but he used my learning how to love him more to teach my kids to love him more too.

As I conclude this book, I have one last secret I want to share with you. I'm a little afraid to pour so much of myself into this book and launch it into this big, bad world. But I believe God will use my vulnerable weakness to help you grow in your faith.

Do you remember the night I tucked our Big Joe into his top bunk, and he said, "I love you more?" Well, he's a super-sensitive guy, so on the days I have a tough day writing, he can feel it in me. He senses it. So on these days, my cute freckled boy follows me around, sits beside me, or puts his hand on my back, and we have this conversation moment after moment, day after day . . . for as long as he thinks I need it.

Jo: "Guess what?"

Me: "What Big Jo?"

Jo: "I love you."

Me: "I love you too, JoJo."

Jo: "But Mama, I love you more."

A big grin always comes across my face.

This last Sunday morning, wisdom flowed out of my husband's mouth when he was preaching. "Satan can't steal your eternal life, but he can wreck your abundant life." Life is full of trouble, but we don't have to let Satan make us a wreck because of it. John 10:10 says, "The thief comes to steal and kill and destroy; I have come that they may have life, and have it to the full."

I wrote this book because I don't want you to get stuck. Don't let Satan steal Jesus' love and joy from you. Fight for the abundant life Jesus has promised by loving him more. Don't give up. Keep moving forward, even if moving forward simply means you stand your ground. Jesus died to give you life . . . life to the full. So when you feel down, think of my JoJo putting his hand on my back and telling me he loves me because I imagine this is just what Jesus is doing for you. He is with you, reminding you over and over and over again that *he loves you more*.

ENDNOTES

CHAPTER 1

1. Neil Anderson with Hyatt Moore, *In Search of the Source: First Encounter with God's Word* (Orlando: Wycliffe Bible Translators, 1999), 44-45.

2. Neil Anderson with Hyatt Moore, *In Search of the Source: First Encounter with God's Word* (Orlando: Wycliffe Bible Translators, 1999), 45-46.

3. NewSpring Worship, "Oh My God, My Father," Salvation Rise, 2014.

4. Quang Nhuong Huynh, *The Land I Lost: Adventures of a Boy in Vietnam* (New York: Harper Trophy, 1982), 104-105.

CHAPTER 2:

5. Beth Moore, *Paul, 90 Days on His Journey of Faith* (Nashville: B&H Publishing Group, 2010), 188-189.

CHAPTER 3:

6. Mike Foster, *People of the Second Chance: A Guide to Bringing Life-Saving Love to the World* (Colorado Springs: WaterBrook Multnomah, 2016), 30.

7. Mike Foster, *People of the Second Chance: A Guide to Bringing Life-Saving Love to the World* (Colorado Springs: WaterBrook Multnomah, 2016), 19.

8. Lisa Whittle, *Put Your Warrior Boots On: Walking Jesus Strong, Once and For All* (Eugene: Harvest House Publishers, 2017), 51-52.

9. Mary Demuth, *The Wall Around Your Heart: How Jesus Heals You When Others Hurt You* (Nashville: Nelson Books, 2013), 140.

10. Mike Foster, *People of the Second Chance: A Guide to Bringing Life-Saving Love to the World* (Colorado Springs: WaterBrook Multnomah, 2016), Forward.

CHAPTER 4:

11 . D. Jeanene Watson, *Teresa of Calcutta: Serving the Poorest of the Poor* (Fenton: Mott Media Publishing, 1984), 72-73.

12. D. Jeanene Watson, *Teresa of Calcutta: Serving the Poorest of the Poor* (Fenton: Mott Media Publishing, 1984), 74.

CHAPTER 6:

13. https://newspring.cc/stories/jackie-jeter

14. https://newspring.cc/stories/jackie-jeter

15. https://vimeo.com/52641844, https://newspring.cc/stories/trish-crossley

16. Lewis Smedes, *The Art of Forgiving: When You Need to*

Forgive and Don't Know How (New York: Ballentine Books, 1996), 43.

17. Lewis Smedes, *The Art of Forgiving: When You Need to Forgive and Don't Know How* (New York: Ballentine Books, 1996), 117.

CHAPTER 7:

18. Joanna Weaver, *Having a Mary Heart in a Martha World: Finding Intimacy with God in the Busyness of Life* (Colorado Springs: WaterBrook and Multnomah, 2009), 137-138.

ACKNOWLEDGEMENTS

"Impossible is where God starts. Miracles are what God does. The ingredients for a miracle are always in our midst. Anything that God asks us to do is impossible. If we can do it, then we don't need God. The impossible makes us rely on God so that it's literally impossible for us to take the credit."
— Christine Caine, Catalyst Conference 2015

This book is truly a miracle. It has felt impossible for so many reasons. But there is someone who has believed and supported me through all my ups and downs, prayed for me, and let me read every chapter to him out loud. This special someone is the greatest gift God has ever given me . . . my husband. Thank you, Clayton, for loving me tirelessly. I couldn't have written this book without your encouragement.

Also, to my children, Jacob and Joseph. Thank you for encouraging me every time I left the house to write. Thank you for always saying, "You can do it, Mama. We believe in you." I love you both. You are two sweet treasures.

Friends, I am scared to start listing your names because my brain feels like mush, and I don't want to forget any of you. So if you think this thank you is to you, it is. Thanks for the prayers, texts, and words of encouragement. I couldn't have done it without you.

SHARIE KING

SPEAKER · AUTHOR · PASTOR'S WIFE

Helping Women
MOVE FORWARD
in their
FAITH

LEARN MORE AT WWW.SHARIEKING.COM

and follow her on social media

  HTTPS://WWW.FACEBOOK.COM/SHARIEKING1

  @SHARIEKING99

PARTICIPANT'S GUIDE
COMING SOON

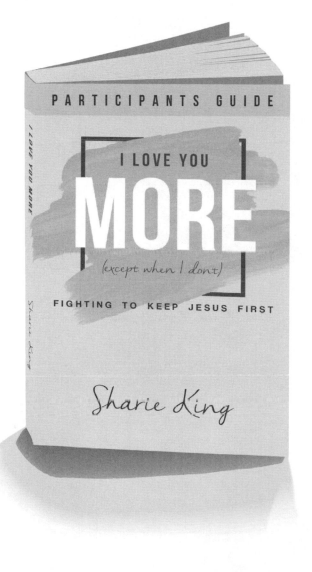

Winner Bakes All

The Cupcake Club

The Cupcake Club

Sheryl Berk and Carrie Berk

SCHOLASTIC INC.

To Elizabeth Maria Walsh:
you are the meaning of champion.
Love,
Care Bear

ISBN 978-0-545-66368-7

12 11 10 9 8 7 6 5 4 3 2 1   14 15 16 17 18 19/0

Printed in the U.S.A.   40

First Scholastic printing, January 2014

Cover design by Rose Audette

Trouble Times Two

Sadie Harris kicked back on her bed, stretching her long legs up against the wooden headboard. She pitched a pink rubber ball against the wall, catching it effortlessly in her baseball glove, over and over.

"Quit the bouncing," her big brother Tyler shouted. His bedroom was on the other side. "I'm trying to study."

Sadie sighed. She needed to study, too. But she'd been wrestling with her math homework for more than an hour and it just refused to click.

She sat up and flipped open her math notebook. There it was, the still unsolved story problem: "Ms. Erikka had 420 pencils and 112 erasers. She kept 15 pencils and 5 erasers for herself, and now she needs to divide the rest evenly among 30 students. Write an equation and solve."

She stared at the question and it stared back at her, daring her to start writing. She had no clue where to begin. *Why does Ms. Erikka have so many pencils and erasers? And honestly, couldn't each student just take one and leave the extras in the supply basket? Did they have to make things so complicated?*

Sadie hated math. She hated it more than getting a cavity filled at the dentist. She hated it more than missing a jump shot in a basketball game. She couldn't explain it, but math made her feel all topsy-turvy inside. The bigger the equation, the more she panicked—and in fifth grade, the equations were *humongous*! As if that wasn't bad enough, her dyslexia often flipped the numbers around, so she had to really concentrate and check her answers two or three times to make sure she hadn't misread the numbers in the problem.

Her teacher, Ms. Erikka, was very patient with her. She gave Sadie extra time on tests and worked with her privately after class. But nothing seemed to help. "Math-phobia" is what Tyler called it. He had it in fifth grade, too.

"I couldn't add two plus two," he said, illustrating his point with four chocolate-chip cookies plucked out of the jar onto the kitchen counter.

"So how did you learn?" Sadie asked.

"I'm not sure," he replied. "One day in high school, we started learning geometry, and it all made sense to me. Like magic or something."

"Or something." Sadie chuckled.

"No, I'm serious. It was like someone flipped a switch in my brain and the numbers all made sense!"

Sadie nodded. It sounded crazy, but Ty had gotten a 97 on his last calculus test. She could see it tacked to the fridge with big red letters scribbled on top of the sheet that read, "Good job!"

Sadie doubted her math tests would ever have those happy red letters on them.

"You'll see," her mom assured her. "One day you'll just get it and you'll love math."

Love math? She seriously doubted it. There were things she was definitely good at, and math wasn't one of them. Sink a jump shot from the foul line...not a prob! Hit a home run with the bases loaded...piece of cake.

She'd even become an expert at baking, thanks to the cupcake club she and her friends Kylie Carson, Jenna Medina, and Lexi Poole had started the year before in fourth grade. In the beginning, she could barely read a recipe. Now she knew how to whip up a chocolate ganache from scratch and what the difference was between baking powder and baking soda.

"Some people are just born geniuses," her brother Corey

bragged. Sadie had to admit things did come fairly easily to him. Not only had he been the captain of his middle school basketball team, but now—in just the first few weeks of high school—he had managed to land a spot on the football squad.

"When ya got it…ya got it," Corey teased. "And I got it big-time!"

"Yeah, and that matches those big feet!" Tyler countered, pointing to Corey's size 13EEE high-tops.

"Shaquille O'Neal wears a size twenty-two shoe," Corey replied.

"Does that mean you have more growing to do?" Mrs. Harris sighed. "I just bought you new Nikes!"

Sadie giggled. Her brothers reminded her of one of those old-time comedy duos—Laurel and Hardy or Abbott and Costello. Or maybe even Phineas and Ferb? They were always trying to one-up each other. But if there was one thing *she* topped both of her brothers at, it was height.

At ten years old, she stood five feet, five inches tall—head and shoulders above her classmates at Blakely Elementary. When Corey and Tyler were her age, they barely measured five feet. Sadie loved to look at the lines the Harris siblings had made on the basement wall, marking their height at every birthday. She was clearly the height champion for her age.

"You just sprung up like a beanstalk!" her mom told her. "Your brothers didn't have their growth spurts 'til middle school."

"But look at us now!" Tyler pointed out. "I'm six feet, two inches!"

"I hope Sadie doesn't get taller than that!" her mom fretted. "We'll need higher ceilings!"

Some of the kids at Blakely teased her about being so tall. Meredith Mitchell (Blakely's resident bully) loved to call her "Big Foot" and "Gigantua."

"How's the weather up there?" Meredith taunted her when they lined up to go to recess. Jack Yu cracked up: "Yeah, Sadie always has her head in the clouds!"

"Doesn't that bother you?" Kylie once asked her.

"Nope. I just think of Meredith as this teeny, tiny mosquito," Sadie told her. "Buzz…buzz…SPLAT!" She swatted the air and made Kylie crack up. "Besides, I kick her butt every time we're in P.E. She's all mouth…no game."

Even her coach had a "tall" nickname for Sadie: "Hey, Stretch! Let me see that defense!" The fact that people noticed her height never bothered Sadie. She was proud to be "Stretch Harris." Her brothers were tall. Her mom and dad were tall. In fact, almost everyone in the Harris family had the tall gene.

"Your grandpa Willie was six feet, five inches," her mother told her. "He would bump his head whenever he came through our door."

Sadie remembered her Papa Willie as a kind, gentle man, and she loved to look up to him when she was a little girl. It never bothered him if he had to duck while getting out of a car, and it never bothered her if she had to hug her knees when she sat in a crowded row in the movies.

But algebra was another story. *That* bothered Sadie big-time! Especially when Ms. Erikka called on her in class.

"Sadie, if 2 times n equals 96, what is n?" her teacher asked.

Sadie stared at the SMART Board, hoping for a number to magically materialize. No such luck. Couldn't she have a fairy godmother with a Magic Marker wand to give her a hint?

"Um…uh…I don't know," Sadie sighed.

"Well, take a guess!" Ms. Erikka encouraged her.

"Um, 18? 24? 36?" The class erupted in giggles.

"Can you tell us how you got those answers?" her teacher asked.

"Well, you told me to guess…" Sadie replied.

"A mathematical guess," Ms. Erikka corrected her. "One that's based on mathematical reasoning. Like what number doubled would give you 96?"

Sadie was still stumped. She had no idea what her teacher was talking about.

"Ooh, ooh! I know! It's 48!" Meredith waved her hand wildly in the air.

"No calling out, but, yes, thank you, Meredith, the answer is 48. Sadie, do you see how we got that?"

Sadie smiled and nodded, but what she was really thinking was, "I have no idea!"

☆ ☮ ☆

She also had no clue how to solve this math homework problem about the pencils and erasers. She flopped back down on her bed and buried her head in her basketball pillow. If she failed math, the coach would kick her off the Blakely Bears. His rule was simple: no pass, no play.

Her teammates would never forgive her because she was the best chance they had for making the state championships this year. They knew it, and she knew it, so why wouldn't her brain cooperate? Why couldn't she just make those multiplication and division tables stick?

Suddenly, her cell phone rang and she dove for it on her desk. She recognized the number instantly. It was Kylie.

"What's the answer to question number 4?" she blurted out.

"What ever happened to 'Hey, girl? What's up?'" Kylie teased. "Is that how you talk to all the members of our cupcake club?"

"Nope…just the one who got a ninety-nine on the last math test. Seriously, Kylie, I'm stuck. I really need your help!"

"No sweat! I can come over—I wanted to try out a new recipe for white chocolate cupcakes anyway."

Her friend had a one-track brain, and it always led straight to cupcakes. That's why Kylie was president of their business, Peace, Love, and Cupcakes. She kept Sadie, Jenna, and Lexi up to their ears in flour and frosting every week.

"I dunno, Kylie," Sadie groaned. She glanced over at the dozens of trophies lined up on the shelf over her desk: basketball, track, soccer, softball. Her dad called it her "Wall of Fame." But the one prize she *really* wanted she hadn't won yet: the Elementary School Basketball State Championship cup. If it was up to Kylie, she'd have Sadie baking all afternoon—and they'd get so wrapped up in cupcakes that Sadie would forget all about her math quiz.

"I'll make you a deal," she bargained with Kylie. "You help me with my homework, and *then* we'll hit the mixer."

"Yay! I'll send Lexi and Jenna a text and tell them to come to your house," Kylie replied.

"I better make sure it's cool with my mom—hang on!" Sadie opened her bedroom door and shouted, "Hey, Mom! Is it okay if the cupcake club holds a taste test in our kitchen?"

She heard her mom's voice, but she couldn't make out what she was saying.

"What? I can't hear you!" Sadie called.

She climbed down a few steps on the staircase to get a better listen—and then realized her mom was talking to her dad, not to her.

"Ty needed new jeans, and Sadie's sneakers are too small! And Corey…well, he's growing out of everything…"

"You charged $300 on the Am Ex?" her father yelled. "We have to tighten the purse strings, Bria, not spend every cent we have on things we don't need."

"What would you like me to do, Gabe? Send your kids to school *barefoot*?"

Sadie gulped. They both sounded so angry at each other. She tiptoed back to her room and picked up her phone.

"I don't know if it's a good time," she told Kylie.

"What do you mean? It's always a good time to bake cupcakes!" Kylie insisted.

"It's just my parents…they're having a fight."

"Oh," Kylie said softly. "What about?"

"Money, I guess," Sadie sighed. "My dad's contracting business is pretty slow. He says it's because the economy is bad right now. No one is building or redecorating, so he doesn't have much work."

"Well, do you want to come over here instead?" Kylie offered.

Through her open door, Sadie could still hear her parents arguing. Getting out of the house sounded really good at the moment. She hated to think of her mom and dad fighting. But it was happening more and more lately—and it made Sadie worry. Her mom and dad couldn't seem to speak to each other anymore without getting angry.

Last night's disagreement had been one of the worst, and there wasn't any arguing involved. Over dinner, her father had announced there was no money to go on a ski trip over winter break this year.

"Aw, you're kidding me!" Corey moaned. "We always go skiing in Colorado."

"Well, not this year. Sorry," her dad replied. Sadie

noticed that her mother was looking down at her dinner plate, not saying a word.

"Can't we go for just a few days?" Tyler whined. "I was really looking forward to skiing the back bowls this year."

"This discussion is over," her dad snapped. "Next year."

"So what will we do over winter break?" Sadie asked. She knew most of her friends would be away for the holidays. Kylie's parents were taking her to Florida to visit her cousins, and Lexi had tickets to see the Radio City Christmas show with her Aunt Dee in New York.

"I was thinking you could visit Gram and Pops in Poughkeepsie," her dad said.

"*Poughkeepsie?*" Corey gasped. "What the heck do you do in Poughkeepsie for a week?"

Her mom finally spoke up. "There are some lovely museums."

Tyler made a face. "Yeah, that sounds like a whole lotta fun…"

"Pops is like a hundred years old," Corey groaned. "He only wants to watch old kung fu movies on TV. They don't even speak English in them. It's torture!"

"Hah-*yah*!" Sadie giggled, pretending to karate-chop her brother.

Just then, her mother rose from the table, slamming her plate into the sink. She was just as disappointed as they were. Sadie could feel it.

"I don't want to cancel our trip, but I have no choice," her dad tried to explain. "The airfare, the hotel, the meals, the ski rentals. How could we possibly afford it?"

Her mom stormed out of the kitchen and refused to say another word to her father all night. "The silent treatment" was what Tyler called it. "It's when she's super mad, so mad she can't even talk," he whispered. "This is *baaad*."

It was bad. Very bad. And Sadie didn't know how to explain all of this to Kylie. Her mom and dad argued once in a while—usually over silly things, like who forgot to close the garage door. It was nothing like this.

"Kylie, do you think my parents will get divorced?" Sadie asked softly. She knew her friend would give her a straight answer.

"Um, I don't know, Sadie. How bad are they fighting?"

Sadie filled Kylie in on yesterday's and today's fireworks.

There was silence on the other end of the phone. Sadie knew Kylie was thinking hard before she gave an answer.

"Well, lots of kids at Blakely Elementary have divorced

parents," she finally replied. Sadie thought that was her nice way of saying, "Yeah, it's a definite possibility."

"But I don't want mine to be divorced. It's awful! You live in two houses and have two rooms. You're always going back and forth…"

"Hey, don't frost the cupcake before it's cooled!" Kylie interrupted.

Sadie scratched her head. "What does that mean?"

"It means 'Don't think too fast.' Your parents haven't told you they're getting divorced!"

Sadie shook the ugly idea of divorce out of her head and tried to focus instead on happier thoughts—like spending the afternoon with the cupcake club and finishing her math homework in time to watch the Giants game on TV tonight. "Okay, I'll come over."

"Awesome!" Kylie cheered. Then she added gently, "Whatever happens, Sadie, you know we're all here for you, right?"

☆ ☮ ☆

Sadie *did* know Kylie, Jenna, and Lexi would always stand by her. She remembered the time last year when she sprained her ankle and was on crutches for two weeks. She thought it was the end of the world, but the girls assured her it was only a temporary setback. She'd be back in the game in no time.

"It's like in *The Mummy Returns*," Kylie explained. "They think the mummy is gone for good…but no! He wakes up again to terrorize Brendan Fraser!"

Sadie rolled her eyes. "This is basketball, Kylie, not a monster movie."

"Kylie has a point," Lexi insisted. "The doctor said you'd be fine in two weeks."

"Two weeks!" Sadie moaned, gently touching her bandaged ankle. "I have to walk around on crutches! How am I supposed to go up and down the stairs at school?"

"Piggyback ride?" Jenna joked. "Or we could tie a rope around your waist and pull you up the side of the building through the science lab window…"

Sadie was moping for two days straight until the girls showed up at her doorstep with a plan to cheer her up.

"Cupcake delivery!" they announced when Mrs. Harris answered the door.

"Oh, my…come right in, girls. She's in the living room. Just be careful: she's not in a great mood and she bites!"

When Sadie turned around, she couldn't believe her eyes.

There were Kylie, Jenna, and Lexi, all dressed like giant cupcakes with silver foil wrappers around their hips and red "cherry" balloons tied to their heads. Each girl was wearing a white T-shirt "sprinkled" with multicolored specks of paint.

"Special delivery for Sadie Harris!" Jenna giggled. "A singing cupcake-gram!"

Kylie hit the Play button on her iPod touch, and hip-hop music filled the living room. The trio began to rap:

"Sadie, Sadie, don't be blue!
We've got a cupcake-gram for you!
What's tall and cool and super sweet?
Can you guess who'll be back on her feet?
Sadie, Sadie, give a cheer!
You'll get well soon, we have no fear!"

At the end of the rap, Kylie and Jenna got down on their hands and knees, and Lexi climbed on their backs, forming a pyramid. She wobbled but managed to stand up and toss confetti in the air. "Hugs and sprinkles from PLC!" all three shouted, showering the couch—and Sadie—with glittering shreds of paper.

Sadie and her mom applauded wildly. "That was amazing, girls," her mother said. "Love the costumes!"

Lexi climbed down. "Aren't they cool? It was my idea to do the cherries on top." She took off the balloon and handed it to Sadie. "At least we got you to smile!"

Sadie had to admit that she did feel better. They'd even baked her get-well cupcakes with cute little fondant crutches on top.

"This is really nice of you," she said, licking the chocolate buttercream off her fingers.

"You didn't think we'd let you sit around feeling sorry for yourself, did you?" Kylie asked. "If you can't come to the cupcakes, the cupcakes will come to you!"

☆ ☮ ☆

Sadie would never forget how the girls had managed to take her mind off her troubles. But divorce wasn't as simple to fix as a sprained ankle. And no amount of cupcakes could help her pass fifth-grade math if she failed her quiz this week. What would she do? What *could* she do?

Kylie read her mind. "We'll work it out," she assured Sadie.

Let It Snow!

"We need to come up with a new cupcake of the month," Kylie told her fellow PLC-ers. "Something that's wintery." They had spread dozens of cookbooks on Kylie's bed and were flipping through the pages, searching for ideas.

"What about angel food cake...with snow angels on top?" Lexi suggested, holding up her notebook. Sadie checked out her sketch: it was beautifully drawn as always, and the cupcakes looked heavenly.

"I'm thinking candy cane cupcakes—with peppermint frosting," Jenna piped up. "Or what about hot cocoa cupcakes...with mini marshmallows? You know me...it's all about the flavor."

"I think those are all cool," Kylie agreed. "Especially with the forecast this week. They're predicting a major blizzard in the Northeast."

"Can you say, 'Snow Day'?" Jenna exclaimed. "I have

this awesome flying saucer sled. *Vamos a la nieve!* Let it snow!"

"Snowball fight!" Kylie chimed in. "You are so going down, Jenna!"

"I'm just hoping it hits before Friday's math quiz," Sadie added. "Don't you think they'll close school if we get a foot of snow?"

"Probably, and that will give us a chance to work on our designs," Lexi said, getting down to cupcake business. She grabbed her sketchbook and began drawing. "What if we sprinkled the top of a white chocolate cupcake with shredded coconut to look like a snowball?" She held up her sketch.

"Mr. Ludwig will love those for the Golden Spoon," Kylie said. "Snowball cupcakes in honor of the blizzard!" The girls knew their steady customer would want a brand-new batch of cupcakes to sell in his gourmet shop in Greenwich as soon as possible. He'd already left Kylie two messages asking when he could get his delivery this week.

He was a loyal friend to Peace, Love, and Cupcakes. After all, he'd given them their very first business contract after sampling one of their chocolate cupcakes at a school event. Thanks to Mr. Ludwig, they had become more than just a Blakely Elementary School cupcake club. They were now a real baking business. But he wasn't the most patient person on the planet!

"Maybe we should send out an email blast," Jenna pointed out. "Let our customers know we've got new flavors. It might help our business pick up a little…"

Kylie flipped through their accounting log. Jenna was right. They had been selling five or six dozen fewer every week. Even Mr. Ludwig had reduced his weekly order from 300 to 240 cupcakes, and just this past weekend they'd had a birthday order cancellation at the last minute.

"I think it's the economy," Sadie said. "My dad says things are tough all over."

Jenna nodded. "You can say that again."

"Is your family okay?" Sadie had almost forgotten that Ms. Medina was a single mom with five kids. Jenna's family didn't have a lot of money to begin with, and her mom relied heavily on her job in a tailor shop.

"My mom says people always need their clothes sewn and hemmed. The less new stuff you can afford to buy, the more you have to fix what you have. She and my two older sisters have been pretty busy lately."

Sadie was relieved. At least someone was doing well. She wished she could say the same for her family. She didn't dare tell her parents that her basketball coach had mentioned buying new team uniforms this year. They'd freak because the uniform would cost a fortune.

"Maybe your mom could get a job as a seamstress," Jenna suggested.

Sadie chuckled at the thought. Her mom couldn't even sew on a button. Last year, Sadie had torn her track shorts before a meet and asked her mom to sew them. Her mom had no idea what to do with a needle and thread, so she'd used a stapler and tape to repair the shorts. Just as Sadie crossed the finish line, she heard "*Rip!*" and felt a draft. She didn't realize what had happened until the track team captain pointed to her butt and giggled, "Nice polka-dot panties!"

"I don't think my mom is the sewing type," Sadie reflected.

"Well, what is she good at?" Lexi asked. "She must be good at something."

Sadie twirled her ponytail. "Well, she's good at being a mom. She always says it's the best job anyone could ever have."

"That's true," Lexi replied, "but it doesn't pay much, does it?"

"Maybe you could help. Do some baby-sitting on the side," Kylie offered.

Sadie already felt like she had three full-time jobs: the

cupcake club, the basketball team, and being a fifth-grader. She couldn't imagine piling more on her plate, but she felt like she needed to do something to help her family.

"We're just going to have to make more money with PLC," she told her friends. "I think the more money my family has, the less my parents will fight."

She noticed that Kylie had been awfully quiet this whole time—which usually meant she was cooking up a crazy cupcake plan.

"Kylie?" Sadie tapped her friend on the shoulder. "What are you thinking?"

"I got it!" Kylie spun around in her desk chair. "Peace, Love, and Cupcakes Points!"

Sadie raised an eyebrow. "Points? Points for what? Like a video game?"

"It's like the frequent-shopper cards my mom uses at the pharmacy and the grocery store," Kylie explained. "For every cupcake you buy, you collect points until you earn enough to get a dozen free. In our case, if you buy three dozen cupcakes in a month, you get one dozen free."

"That's a great idea, Kylie!" Lexi exclaimed. "People will order from us every week to earn their cupcake points. We'll have tons of orders!"

"And tons of deliveries to make," Jenna pointed out. "What do we do about that?"

"Tyler and Corey will help with the deliveries," Sadie volunteered. She knew she could convince them—especially if it helped make peace between their parents.

"Maybe we should paint Tyler's car to look like a cupcake-mobile," Lexi suggested. "Cupcake trucks are really popular in New York City. I saw a lot of them there when I was staying with Aunt Dee."

Sadie shook her head. "I don't think my brother would appreciate that. He thinks his Honda is a 'babe magnet.'" The girls all giggled.

"What should we say in the email subject line?" Kylie asked. She opened her laptop and began typing.

"What about 'Get to the point!'" Jenna joked. "As in PLC Points."

Sadie thought about what would get her attention in an email. "How about, 'Sweet Rewards: Free Cupcakes for PLC Customers!'"

"Love it!" Kylie high-fived her. "This is going to be our biggest selling week ever!"

A Storm Is Brewing

The next day at school, the girls needed to run their plan by Juliette Dubois, PLC's advisor and Blakely's drama teacher. Juliette was always very practical with her advice for their business—but she also encouraged them to think big.

"A points program makes a lot of sense," she said. "Everyone is looking for bargains right now. I've been clipping coupons trying to save money myself. And you'll learn a very important lesson: creating customer loyalty will mean long-term sales."

Kylie showed her their idea for the email blast.

"So how long do you intend to run this points program?" Juliette asked.

"We hadn't really thought about that," Sadie answered. "I guess we could run it for a month."

"I think you might need longer than that to get people

hooked," Juliette considered. "I'd say give it a try for three months and see how it does. When are you sending out the email blast—and to how many customers?"

Kylie gulped. "Wow. We didn't think about that either. I guess our entire customer list—that's 500 people. We could get it out tomorrow so people could order for the weekend."

"Now that's a plan, man!" Juliette cheered. "Go to it, girls!"

A day later, the club was flooded with requests for PLC's Cupcake of the Week: "There's No Business like Snow Business." The girls gathered at Sadie's house to bake, decorate, and box the orders so her brothers could deliver them.

"I am totally going to fail my math quiz Friday," Sadie sighed. "With all of this baking, how will I study?"

"We'll bake *and* study," Kylie insisted.

Jenna held up her hands, which were covered in flour and buttercream. "Um, I wouldn't bring any math textbooks in this kitchen at the moment. It's a mess!"

"You see?" Sadie said. "It's hopeless."

"Relax and focus on cupcake math," Kylie insisted.

Lexi giggled. "Now that would be a cool subject in school! Do you get to frost as you do your fractions?"

Kylie continued: "Sadie, we have a total of 216 cupcakes to bake and have four dozen already in the oven. How many do we have left to bake?"

Sadie thought hard and tried to picture the equation in her head. "Well, 4 times 12 equals 48," she began. "So 216 minus 48 would be 168."

Kylie applauded. "And how many dozen is that? Write an equation and solve!"

Sadie closed her eyes and saw cupcakes lined up on a countertop. She pictured them in groups of 12. The equation would be: 168 divided by 12 equals x. So x would be 14.

"We have 14 dozen left to go!" Sadie answered.

"*Muy bueno*!" Jenna cheered. "You are so going to pass that quiz Friday!"

A few flakes started falling outside the window just as the girls were putting the cupcakes in the oven. But by the time the last dozen were piped with white chocolate frosting and dipped in shredded coconut, the winds were whipping up and the ground was covered by a white blanket of snow.

"I thought they didn't say snow 'til Thursday night," Lexi said, peering outside.

"That's weathermen for you," Mrs. Harris sighed. "I guess they were off by a day." She looked concerned.

"Now your father is going to have to stop working on the Saperstones' garage door. It's getting bad out there quickly."

Kylie peered out the window. "I don't think I can bike home in this…"

Mrs. Harris nodded. "I think you should all call your parents and tell them you'll be sleeping over here tonight. We'll see how bad it is in the morning."

Kylie, Jenna, and Lexi cheered: "Slumber party!"

"Better not let my brothers hear that…" Sadie warned. She knew Corey and Tyler would be up to all sorts of tricks if they heard her friends were staying over.

But it was too late. "I smell something good…Hand it over!" Corey demanded. He bounded into the kitchen, tracking snow across the floor, and dropped his dripping wet jacket over the back of a chair.

"Say *please*," Mrs. Harris corrected him.

"Okay…*please* hand it over," Corey joked.

Jenna offered him a cupcake, and he inhaled it in two bites. "Would you like to know what you just ate?" she asked.

"Nope. Just give me another one…" He licked his lips. "Or I will torture you guys all night with practical jokes. Did I ever tell you about the itching powder I put in Sadie's sleeping bag when she was eight?"

The girls looked at Sadie for confirmation. "Give him another cupcake," she said. "I itched for days."

"I hope the snow doesn't shut down all the roads," Kylie suddenly thought. "How will we get all these cupcakes delivered?"

"Dogsled?" Corey teased, helping himself to a third cupcake. "Mush! Mush!"

"Nah...reindeer are better," called a voice from the living room. "On Donner, on Blitzen..." Sadie's brother Tyler appeared in the kitchen, covered in snow. "It's really coming down out there." He scooped a cupcake off the counter and popped it whole in his mouth.

Kylie, Jenna, and Lexi all stared.

"Don't look so surprised," Sadie teased. "My big brothers are human vacuum cleaners. They eat anything that's not nailed down."

Tyler swallowed and let out a huge burp. "Yes, siree, that's me!" He was starting to grab another cupcake when Mrs. Harris swatted his hand away.

"Enough, you two! You'll spoil your dinner. Go get changed and washed up. And girls, let's get this kitchen clean. I know there must be a table somewhere under all that shredded coconut."

Kylie grabbed a broom and helped Sadie sweep the floor. "So…your family seems okay?" she whispered.

Sadie shrugged. "I guess…for now."

☆ ☮ ☆

Sadie's father finally arrived home nearly two hours later. The roads were iced over, and his truck could barely make its way up the steep hill to their house.

"What a night!" he exclaimed as he opened the front door. His black mustache and beard were white with snow.

"Daddy!" Sadie raced to give him a hug. "I was getting worried!"

"What's that? A fraidy Sadie? I never heard of such a thing!" he teased.

Sadie shivered. "Your nose feels like a Popsicle!"

"I was out in the snow for over an hour trying to fix the Saperstones' garage door opener."

"Did you see Jeremy?" Lexi piped up, eager to hear news about her "boyfriend," the Saperstones' youngest son.

"You mean your Romeo?" Jenna teased, referring to the Shakespeare play, *Romeo and Juliet*, they had performed in drama class.

"Jeremy's snowed in just like you ladies," Mr. Harris

said. "Chess practice canceled or something like that." He brushed the snow off the bottoms of his jeans.

"Ooh! I'll go call him now!" Lexi squealed. Sadie rolled her eyes. She couldn't understand how Lexi could care so much about a boy. Sadie had a house full of them…and it was no big deal!

"Did you finish the Saperstones' door?" Mrs. Harris asked hopefully.

He shook his head. "No. I have to do more work on it when this storm blows over."

Sadie guessed that meant no pay for his work today. She tried to wipe the look of disappointment off his face.

"Eskimo kiss!" she said, rubbing noses. "With a real, live Eskimo!"

He smiled, but Sadie saw that her mom was frowning. "I'll reheat your dinner, Gabe," she said, and shuffled back to the kitchen.

※ ◎ ※

Later that evening, Jenna and Lexi made themselves comfy in sleeping bags on the living-room rug while Kylie and Sadie shared the foldout couch. Sadie flipped channels until she found Connecticut's *Battle of the Bakers*. "I want the old lady from Beacon Falls to win tonight's battle," Jenna said, stuffing a handful of popcorn in her mouth. "Go, Granny Annie's Cupcakes!"

"How cool would it be to be on this show?" Kylie day-dreamed. "We could totally win, you know. And the prize is $5,000!"

Lexi thought it over. "We might have a chance. But first you have to make an audition video and send it in."

"So let's make a video!" Kylie insisted. "We could do it tomorrow—I bet there'll be no school. Maybe not even Thursday or Friday."

"Uh, are you forgetting something? Our cupcake deliveries?" Sadie pointed to the boxes piled high on the dining-room table. "No deliveries, no money."

"I'm sure they'll plow the roads by midday, and your brothers will be able to drive them over," Lexi said.

"I need more popcorn for Round 2," Jenna said, waving the empty bowl. "Would ya mind, Sadie?"

Sadie took the bowl and was about to barge into the kitchen when the sound of low, angry voices stopped her. She put her ear against the door and heard her parents. They were at it again.

"I worked all day for nothing!" her father snapped.

"Well, that's not my fault!" her mother barked back.

Sadie couldn't stand it anymore. Why were they always bickering? Why couldn't they get along?

"Hey, Sadie…where's that popcorn? Commercial's over!" Jenna called.

Kylie was the one who noticed Sadie frozen at the kitchen door, clutching the bowl to her chest and eavesdropping. "You okay, Sadie?" she called.

Just then, the tears welled in the corners of her eyes and Sadie couldn't stop them from spilling down her cheeks. She didn't want her friends to think she was a baby, but she couldn't help crying. She felt like her heart was breaking in two.

"No, I'm not okay!" she sobbed, flinging the empty bowl to the floor. "My parents are getting a divorce!"

Lights, Camera, Cupcakes!

Sadie's friends tried to calm her down, but it was no use. She was inconsolable.

"I think you should talk to your parents and tell them how worried you are," Kylie told her.

No way! The last thing she needed tonight was more family drama. She was grateful when her mom went upstairs and slammed the door to her bedroom while her father retreated to his home office. Neither of them noticed how upset *she* was or suspected she had overheard.

"Even if your parents do split up, it'll be okay," Jenna insisted. "My mom does a great job raising us all by herself."

"I don't want my parents to split up," Sadie sniffled. "I want us to be the same happy family we were before!"

"Maybe you will be." Lexi put an arm around her. "Maybe things will get better."

"Or maybe they'll get worse…just like the snowstorm!" Sadie replied.

It was after midnight before she finally fell asleep. The girls were all joking and complaining about Jenna's loud snoring, but Sadie found it soothing—kind of like the sound of an electric mixer on low speed. At least it took her mind off her problems.

☆ ☮ ☆

The next morning, the gray storm clouds rolled away to reveal a bright blue sky. Sadie woke up and rubbed her eyes. They felt sore and swollen from crying. She noticed that it was 10 a.m. and she was the only one still in bed. School was closed! The girls were already dressed and in the kitchen, making phone calls and trying to convince Tyler and Corey to drive their cupcakes around the neighborhood. She hoped everyone would be too busy to bring up last night. She wanted to pretend it never happened.

"My car will never make it in two feet of snow," Tyler replied, taking a swig of orange juice from a container in the fridge. "I don't even think Dad's truck could plow through that."

"You're gonna have to wait 'til the roads thaw out," Corey added. He was a freshman in high school and thought he knew everything.

"When will that be?" Kylie asked.

"Oh, I dunno. Maybe May or June?" He chuckled.

"Not funny," Sadie said, shuffling into the kitchen. "We have to get the cupcakes delivered."

Kylie nodded. "Your sis has spoken. Morning, Sadie!"

As Kylie had predicted, school was closed until the roads could reopen. "We're kinda trapped here for a few hours," Lexi filled her in. "Nothing can go out or come in."

"Which means we have the perfect opportunity to make a video for *Battle of the Bakers*," Kylie suggested. "We have it all planned out already—Jenna kept us up with her snoring!"

"I can't help it." Jenna shrugged. "My sister says I sound like a lawn mower."

Sadie interrupted: "Electric mixer, actually. Your snoring put me to sleep."

"Not me!" Lexi complained. "I tried putting the pillow over my head, even putting on my earphones, but she was just too loud!"

"At least we got some great video ideas cooked up!"

Kylie pointed out. She handed Corey her cell phone. "You can film us."

Corey protested: "Do I look like Steven Spielberg to you?"

Sadie smirked. "No prob, Core. I guess I'll just have to tell Mom how we got that big blue stain on the upstairs rug. Do I need to remind you about your science project accident? The blue Jell-O explosion?"

Her brother winced. "You wouldn't…"

"Wouldn't I?" Sadie batted her eyelashes. She might be the little sister, but she knew how to get her brothers to do what she wanted.

"Go, Sadie!" Kylie laughed. "She shoots! She scores!" She handed the phone to Corey and showed him how to hit Record.

"We're going to start off by introducing ourselves: who we are, and what makes Peace, Love, and Cupcakes so cool," Kylie suggested. She turned to Corey and gave him his cue. "*Action!*"

Tyler snickered. "What are you gonna call your video? The Real Cupcake Bakers of Connecticut? America's Got Cupcakes? Project Cupcakes?"

The girls ignored him. "Hi, I'm Kylie…I'm Jenna…I'm Lexi…I'm Sadie…"

Corey turned the camera to face himself. "And I'm Corey! My sister and her weird friends are shooting this dumb video…"

"Ignore him." Sadie frowned. "We can edit that out. Keep going, Kylie…"

"Together, we are Peace, Love, and Cupcakes—the best cupcake bakers in Connecticut! We're only in fifth grade, and we have our own cupcake business. Just look what we can do!"

She pointed to Lexi, who expertly piped a beautiful rose on top of a cupcake. "First I fill the bag, then I squeeze it like this," she instructed. "Just a little puff of pressure and you've got the perfect petal."

Next, Kylie signaled Sadie who cracked eggs one-handed. "The trick is to make one, firm tap on the bowl with the egg so it cracks cleanly," Sadie explained. "Not a shell in sight!"

Finally, Jenna whipped a flawless lavender buttercream in a mixer. "Always taste your frosting to make sure it's the perfect sweetness and texture," she said. She took a lick of frosting off her pinkie. "*Perfecto!*"

Then all three of them rolled fondant and stamped out the letters PLC and a peace sign and placed them on top of four cupcakes. They each held a cupcake up to the camera and shouted together, "PLC *rocks*!" With that, Tyler snuck up behind them and dumped a bag of flour over Sadie's head.

"Now that's a wrap!" Corey laughed, zooming in for a close-up.

Sadie was about to scream when her mom walked in to see what all the commotion was about.

"Clean it up," she said sternly. "And apologize to your sister. Both of you."

☆ ☮ ☆

Sadie showered and changed and came back downstairs to see the final video Lexi had put together with iMovie on her laptop.

"It's so cool, Lex," Jenna exclaimed. "I love how you put in pics of our best cupcake creations—like the swaying palm tree we made out of mango mini cupcakes. And the giant Ferris wheel that spun rainbow tie-dyed cupcakes. We really look like professional bakers."

"We *are* professional bakers," Kylie insisted. "Which is why we're going to get picked for *Battle of the Bakers*. You'll see!"

Sadie wasn't as convinced, but she liked the sound track

Lexi had spliced in: Gwen Stefani's "The Sweet Escape." She doubted Granny Annie's audition sounded this cool!

"Maybe we can get Mr. Ludwig to say something on camera for us," Kylie added. "Something like, 'Their cupcakes are my best sellers!'"

Jenna groaned. "He'd probably say, 'I discovered them! I take all the credit!' But I guess it's worth a try."

Kylie dialed the number for the Golden Spoon. "That's strange," she said. "It says the number's out of service."

"Maybe the storm downed the phone lines in Greenwich," Mrs. Harris suggested. "The radio says the roads should be open in the next few hours, so maybe Sadie's dad can take you over there with your delivery."

By 3 p.m., the girls were able to pile into Mr. Harris's truck. They strapped the boxes of cupcakes to the flatbed and crossed their fingers that the truck wouldn't skid on the icy roads. Everyone was delighted that PLC was able to deliver—especially a five-year-old girl named Dale who'd been crying all morning.

"I thought my birthday was ruined," she whimpered. Sadie smiled and opened a box to reveal a dozen Rapunzel cupcakes, each with a long braid of orange licorice "hair" on top.

"I love them!" the birthday girl said, hugging Sadie tightly around the knees. "Thank you so, so much!"

"Did you get that for the video?" Sadie winked at Kylie. "Another happy PLC customer!"

Kylie checked her watch—it was nearly 4 p.m. And they'd promised Mr. Ludwig yesterday his delivery would be there by 8 a.m.!

"I don't think our next customer is going to be as happy," she warned. "Mr. Ludwig hates when we're late. And this time, we're super late and couldn't even reach him."

"Hop in, cupcakers," Mr. Harris called. "Next stop... the Golden Spoon."

Golden Opportunity

When Mr. Harris pulled up to the store, there was huge sign out front that read, "CLOSED FOR DISASTER."

"Disaster? What kind of disaster?" Kylie wondered out loud. She knocked on the front door. "Mr. Ludwig? Are you in there?"

"Go away!" said a meek voice. "Can't you read the sign?"

"But we brought you your order!" said Lexi.

"Didn't you hear me? I said GO!" the voice shouted.

"Let's go, girls," Mr. Harris said. "He obviously doesn't want any cupcakes."

"*Wait!*" Sadie shouted. "Mr. Ludwig! It's us, Peace, Love, and Cupcakes!"

The lock slowly turned and the door creaked open. There was Mr. Ludwig, bundled in his coat, hat, and scarf. Sadie thought he looked like she had this morning: all red-eyed and puffy. Had he been crying, too?

"What's wrong?" she asked. "You look awful!"

"What's wrong? Isn't it obvious?" he replied. "There's an enormous hole in my roof, and my entire store is buried under snow and water! I'm ruined!"

Mr. Harris surveyed the huge hole in the roof. "It gave under the weight of the snow," he said. "It's pretty bad but probably fixable." The glass display cases were shattered, all the shelving had fallen off the walls, and the floor was about a foot under water. Mr. Ludwig kept holding his head in his hands, moaning.

"Fixable? I've called everyone in the tristate area, begging them to fix it. No one can get my store open. They're saying it will take months. But to be closed for months—that would be end of the Golden Spoon for sure."

"Does this mean you don't want your 240 cupcakes?" Jenna asked.

Sadie elbowed her in the ribs. "We totally understand, Mr. Ludwig," she replied. "But I know someone who can fix it."

"You do? Who?" Mr. Ludwig's face brightened.

Sadie grabbed her dad's hand and pulled him forward. "Him. My dad. Harris Contracting. He's a great builder."

Mr. Harris looked shocked. "I, um, well, I…" he began.

"Thanks for the vote of confidence, honey, but I don't know if I can fix it."

"Of course you can!" Sadie insisted. "You can fix anything! Remember when PLC built that Statue of Liberty out of key lime cupcakes and her head kept falling off? You totally stuck it on with Gorilla Glue."

"Honey, that was a cupcake sculpture. This is a roof that's been totaled. I can't use Gorilla Glue. I don't even know where to begin."

"Please, Dad," Sadie pleaded. "I'm sure Mr. Ludwig would pay you to fix it fast."

"Oh, yes. If you can get it fixed in a few weeks and I can open my store, I would be so grateful!" Mr. Ludwig begged.

"Pretty please with frosting on top?" Sadie threw in. She knew that a quick paycheck was just what her dad needed—and that might put an end to all the arguing at home.

"I'll have to think about," Mr. Harris said. "I'll let you know tonight."

☆ ☮ ☆

After Mr. Harris dropped Jenna, Lexi, and Kylie off at their homes, Sadie cranked up the car radio and stared out the window. Selena Gomez was singing "Falling Down," and that's exactly how she felt—like the world was falling down around her. She was furious at her father for blowing this "Golden" opportunity. What was wrong with him?

"I know you're angry," he said. Sadie pretended not to hear. "Ignoring me isn't helping."

"Well, you're not helping either!" she fired back. "You and Mom say we have no money. You're always fighting over it. Why wouldn't you take that job?"

"Because I don't make promises I can't keep," her father explained. "Would you take an order for 10,000 cupcakes in two hours if you knew it was impossible to deliver?"

"It's not the same thing," Sadie sniffed.

"No, it's not. Fixing a roof is a major job, honey. What Mr. Ludwig is asking may be impossible. We're not talking a little leak or a few broken shingles. We're talking a giant hole and major water damage. The Golden Spoon is totaled."

"But won't you just try?" Sadie insisted. "How do you know if it's impossible unless you try?"

"I said I'll think about it. I need to take some measurements and get some estimates on the materials."

At least, Sadie thought, he wasn't completely giving up. That was a relief! But she didn't feel much better when her mom told her the roads were open and school would be in session tomorrow. "Everything is back to normal," Mrs. Harris said.

Sadie wished that was true. She used to think her parents were so romantic and "mushy." They held hands at the movies and kissed each other hello and good-bye.

"When I met your father, it was like a bolt of lightning struck me," her mom had confided in her once. "He was handsome, strong, charming. He absolutely swept me off my feet."

What happened between them? Sadie wondered. She looked at their wedding picture on the mantel. Her mom wore an elegant, strapless, white lace gown and veil, and her dad was in a top hat and tails. They looked so in love! When had things started to fall apart?

Sadie suddenly remembered what her dad had told her on the car ride home: "Sometimes you can try and try, but something is just too broken to be fixed."

She gulped. Was he talking about the Golden Spoon's roof....or her parents' marriage? Was that too broken to fix as well? Had he and her mom decided they were done trying?

Sweet Victory

When Friday arrived, Sadie almost forgot about her pop quiz in math. She'd been so worried about her parents, and so angry over the Golden Spoon job, that she hadn't had time to panic over it. Ms. Erikka handed her the test sheet and smiled. "I know you can do it, Sadie," she said. "Just take your time, check your work, and *breathe*."

Sadie remembered how Kylie had told her to picture things instead of numbers. "Make the equation real to you," she'd advised. So when the question asked how many cars were needed to drive forty-five students on a class trip, Sadie pictured her dad driving her and her three friends to the Golden Spoon on Thursday. One driver and four people could fit in each car…that meant they would need nine cars. She got it!

"How do you think you did?" Kylie pulled her aside as the class bell rang.

"Okay," Sadie shrugged. "I'm pretty sure I passed."

"Yay!" Kylie hugged her. "And I have some more good news. Principal Fontina said we could set up a table in the cafeteria with the 240 cupcakes the Golden Spoon couldn't use and sell them—as long as we donated half the money to the Blakely Eco Center."

"Cool," Sadie replied. "So at least we'll make back some money to cover the cost of those ingredients."

"Now on to our next problem," Jenna said, sneaking up behind them in the hall. "What are we going to do without the Golden Spoon's weekly order?"

Sadie hadn't even considered the impact the Golden Spoon closing would have on PLC. Kylie was right: Mr. Ludwig was their biggest customer—and a steady paycheck. Without his business, they'd have to scale back for sure. And that was not what any of them wanted. PLC was going to be even bigger and better this year…they'd promised themselves!

"You have to convince your dad to repair the roof," Jenna said.

"I tried. He won't listen to me." Sadie sighed. "He says it's impossible. He's taking some measurements, but he's convinced it's not going to work."

"Nothing is impossible," Kylie insisted. "I used to think

having a cupcake club was impossible. You used to think learning math was impossible. We've proved everyone wrong, right?"

Sadie thought about it. She had to make her dad see things her way.

"I have an idea," she told Kylie and Jenna. "Meet me at the basketball game tonight—and bring Lexi! We need all the help we can get!"

When she got home, her father was at his desk in the den, crunching numbers on his calculator. He was surrounded by a stack of bills, and Sadie knew he was stressed out. So she treaded lightly.

"Hey, Dad, you coming to my basketball game tonight at the gym?" she asked.

Mr. Harris looked up, happy that Sadie was speaking to him. "Wouldn't miss it for the world, hon." He smiled. "I hear the North Canaan Cougars are a tough team to beat."

"Not for my girl," Mr. Harris said. "You'll cream 'em," he added.

"So you're saying, *nothing* is impossible?"

Mr. Harris looked up from his desk. "What are you up to, Sadie?" he asked.

"Nothing!" Sadie planted a kiss on his cheek.

She raced upstairs to get into her uniform. At the game, she made sure that her PLC members were seated right behind her family on the bleachers. "I'm going to go for a long shot, and when I make it, I want you to make sure to remind my dad: 'Nothing is impossible.' Got that?"

Lexi looked puzzled. "Is that code for something?"

"Yes, it's code for 'Fix Mr. Ludwig's roof!'" Sadie explained. "Just make sure he gets it, okay?"

"Check that," Jenna teased. "Operation Convince Daddy is underway!"

"But, Sadie…what if you miss the shot?" Kylie asked.

"I won't. I can't," Sadie replied.

☆ ☮ ☆

The Blakely Bears were trailing the North Canaan Cougars by one point with only two seconds left in the game. Sadie grabbed the ball and headed down the court. The Cougar defender on her was enormous—at least a head taller than Sadie—and she was waving her arms in the air, blocking Sadie no matter which way she turned. The girl had her completely boxed in.

"She'll never make it!" Lexi cried, covering her eyes. "I can't watch!"

"Go, Sadie!" her father cheered. "You can do it!"

Just then, Sadie faked out the Cougar player. She zigged while defense zagged.

"Go!" screamed her PLC mates. "Go, Sadie, go!"

She broke free and headed down court, straight for the net. But it was still a tough shot from far away.

"It's impossible to sink that," Kylie piped up. "Don't you think, Mr. Harris?"

Sadie threw the ball, and it landed with a swoosh through the hoop. The Bears won the game, and the team lifted Sadie on their shoulders and carried her down the court.

"Woo-hoo! That's my girl!" Mr. Harris cheered. Tyler and Corey fist-pumped each other.

"Wow, so I guess that means *nothing* is impossible. Right, Mr. Harris?" Jenna winked.

Sadie's dad sighed. "Okay, girls. Point taken. You want me to fix the Golden Spoon's roof even if I think it's impossible to fix."

"Who, us?" Kylie replied innocently. "I don't know what you mean…"

Mr. Harris chuckled. "Well, your pal Sadie sure does. She was planning this all along."

Sadie raced to the stands and hugged her family and friends.

"Awesome shot, sis!" her brother Tyler said. "Almost as amazing as my winning basket over the Groton Gators in seventh grade."

"Hey, Dad…" Sadie smiled. "Something to tell me?"

"You won…and you win," her father said. "I'll let Mr. Ludwig know I'll take the job."

Easier Said Than Drawn

Whenever Sadie's cell phone rang at 7 a.m. on a Saturday morning, it was undoubtedly a cupcake emergency.

"Okay, this better be good, Kylie." She yawned and stretched. "I was just in the middle of this awesome dream. I won the WNBA championships, and Michael Jordan was handing me this huge, gold trophy…"

"Rise and shine, Sadie," Kylie chirped. "We have work to do! I just took a huge rush order from Mrs. Lila Vanderwall, president of the New Fairfield Art Society."

"Okay…let me have it. What, when, and how many?" Sadie sighed.

"What you should be asking is how much—as in how much is she willing to pay us to get this order done for a luncheon tomorrow morning. A ton!"

Sadie was suddenly wide awake. "Like how much is a ton?"

"Double our usual price…plus delivery!" Kylie exclaimed.

"OMG! That's awesome! Give me ten minutes to get dressed and grab my apron, and I'll be there!"

When Sadie arrived at Kylie's house, Lexi and Jenna were already in the kitchen.

"This is the plan," Lexi said, handing Sadie a diagram. "We need to do 250 cupcakes celebrating the art society's new exhibit of Moroccan art. Mrs. Vanderwall wants the Moroccan coat of arms on every cupcake. We googled it, and now we need to get rolling on the fondant…"

"We're making ginger spice cupcakes with a ginger mascarpone frosting," Jenna explained. "I'm thinking maybe a pinch of cumin for that authentic Moroccan flavor."

"What should I do?" Sadie said, peeling off her coat and hat, and tying on an apron.

Kylie handed her a carton of eggs. "Get crackin' on that batter!"

The girls needed nearly two hours to perfect the recipe and another two hours to bake and frost the cupcakes. While Jenna and Sadie made sure the cake and frosting had just the right amount of "kick," Kylie and Lexi worked to create a bright yellow, green, and red shield on each cupcake. On either side of the shield were unicorns.

"I think my unicorns need to look more magical," Kylie

suggested, comparing her fondant sculpture to the image they printed off the computer.

Lexi nodded and brushed a unicorn's gold horn with luster dust. "Magical enough for ya?"

After an entire day of baking and decorating, the cupcakes were boxed and ready to be delivered Sunday morning.

"I smell like a Cinnabon." Sadie laughed. "Jenna got more cinnamon on me than in the batter!"

"Well, at least you don't have mascarpone in your hair," Lexi complained.

"Smile and say 'mascarpone cheese,'" Kylie said, snapping a photo on her phone.

☆ ☮ ☆

The next morning, Mr. Harris drove the girls to the art society and the girls began to unload the cupcakes. There were twenty-two boxes, each one delicately packed with tissue paper between the cupcakes to prevent them from bumping around in Mr. Harris's truck.

"I'm so happy to see that you're prompt," Mrs. Vanderwall greeted them. "I wanted to have plenty of time to set the table perfectly. Please follow me."

She led them through a beautiful room filled with

hand-painted Moroccan tiles in shades of turquoise, orange, and gold. Ceramic pots, plates, and lanterns were arranged in a dazzling array of colors and shapes.

"Wow!" Lexi whispered. "This is amazing!"

"I thought we would display the cupcakes on these authentic Moroccan platters," Mrs. Vanderwall explained, showing the girls to a long rectangular table covered in bright linens.

Lexi opened the first box and gently placed a cupcake in the center of a tray. "Perfect!" she said, examining it.

"What on earth? What *is* that?" Mrs. Vanderwall gasped in horror.

"Um, it's a cupcake?" Kylie replied, confused.

"I ordered 250 cupcakes with the Moroccan coat of arms on them," Mrs. Vanderwall shrieked. "That is *not* it!"

"Oh, no," Kylie winced. "I knew I should have made my unicorns look more magical!"

"There are no unicorns on the Moroccan coat of arms!" the woman screamed. She was fanning herself with an exhibit program and turning a bright shade of red.

Lexi shook her head in disbelief. "We must have made a mistake! They all look so much alike! Do you have a Moroccan coat of arms you can show us?"

Mrs. Vanderwall pointed to a huge flag hanging on the wall. There were two lions on it—and no unicorns.

"What you have made is the Scottish coat of arms," Mrs. Vanderwall sputtered. "I will be humiliated at my luncheon!"

"*Dios mío!*" Jenna whispered. "We are in big trouble!"

"It's not a problem…I promise you, we can fix it!" Kylie tried to calm the flustered woman.

"We can?" Sadie whispered. "We only have two hours until the luncheon!"

"We always carry a repair kit with us in case of a cupcake emergency," Lexi explained. "We'll just take off the horns and reshape and paint the unicorns to look like lions."

"I feel faint…I must sit down!" Mrs. Vanderwall moaned. "My luncheon is ruined…I'm disgraced. Whatever shall I tell the Moroccan prime minister's wife?"

"Don't tell her anything!" Kylie pleaded. "Just give us a chance to fix this!"

While the girls did plastic surgery on the unicorns, Sadie mixed red and yellow food coloring to repaint them a golden hue. The girls all brushed on the color with lightning speed and were just finishing the last cupcake as the first guest entered the room.

"What beautiful Moroccan cupcakes," a lady gushed.

"Oh, I'm so relieved to hear you say that." Mrs. Vanderwall reappeared, mopping her brow with an embroidered hankie. "We're so sorry your husband, the prime minister, couldn't be here to join us as well." She gave the girls a dirty look and escorted her distinguished guest around the exhibit.

Sadie looked down at her shirt, pants, sneakers, and hands. Everything was stained with red food coloring. "I look like a ladybug," she groaned.

"Technically, ladybugs are red with black spots," Jenna corrected her. "Just sayin'…"

"Let's just get our check and get out of here," Sadie sighed.

The girls made their way through the crowd to Mrs. Vanderwall, hoping she'd forgive and forget and hand over their $1,200.

"Well, I'm glad everything worked out and you're happy," Kylie said, putting out her hand to get paid.

"Happy? You nearly gave me a heart attack today! I am anything but happy! And I do not intend to pay you one cent for this frightful experience."

"What? You have to pay us!" Sadie cried. "We worked all day on your cupcakes…"

"And they were wrong. I do not pay for mistakes.

Now leave immediately." She turned her back and stomped away.

"I'm so sorry, Sadie," Kylie said, putting her arm around her friend. "I know you were counting on your share of the money."

Not only was she counting on it, she was planning on using it to buy her new basketball uniform.

"Well, it could have been worse…" Jenna said.

"How?" asked Sadie.

"Give me a minute…I'm working on it."

"I got it: we could have made a coat of arms…with arms on it," Kylie joked. "Like an octopus!"

"I have to *hand* it to you!" Jenna laughed.

"You guys are so corny! Get it? Uni-corny?" Lexi giggled.

Sadie couldn't help but laugh, too. "We got no money… but we're still funny!" she added. No cupcake catastrophe could stop the girls of PLC!

The Heat Is On

Mr. Harris and his crew had worked two weeks on the Golden Spoon—and it was still nowhere near ready to reopen.

"We can't patch the broken rafters. We need to start with brand-new decking," Sadie's dad tried to explain to Mr. Ludwig.

"I don't know what that means…and I don't care," Mr. Ludwig moaned. "Just fix it." The entire store was now covered in ugly black tarp, and Mr. Ludwig couldn't bear to see his beautiful Golden Spoon in such a state of disarray.

"Wow," said Sadie when her dad took her to visit the site. "This is one big hot mess, huh?"

Mr. Harris nodded. "You're not kidding, kiddo. This is some fine job you got me into."

☆✌☆

"I think my dad is going to kill me for making him repair the Golden Spoon," Sadie told her friends at lunch the next day at school. "It's taking way longer than he thought."

"Tell me about it," sighed Kylie. "Without Mr. Ludwig's order, we're down about $900 in sales these past two weeks."

"That's not good." Jenna whistled through her teeth. "We can't stay in business unless we get more business."

Sadie had done everything she could. Their only option now was to wait for her dad to finish his work on the Golden Spoon—and hope that its customers came back.

The only good news in her life was her math quiz score.

"An A-minus! Sadie, that's wonderful!" her mother declared when Sadie showed it to her after school. "I'm so proud of you."

"I guess I'll have even more time to study with our cupcake business drying up." Sadie sighed.

"I'm so sorry, honey," her mom said as she hugged her. "I know how much it means to you girls. Maybe it'll bounce back."

Sadie went to her bedroom where she could think. She dribbled a ball on the hardwood floor. It was what she did whenever she was worried or upset.

"Money, math, Mr. Ludwig," she repeated with each bounce of the ball. "Mom, Dad, divorce. Peace, Love, Cupcakes."

She threw the ball, and it bounced off the back of her door, just missing the net. She was about to take another shot when her iPod touch rang. It was Kylie calling her on FaceTime.

"Put that ball down, Sadie...we're going to battle!"

"Huh?" Sadie asked. "What are you talking about?"

"Remember that video we sent in auditioning for *Battle of the Bakers*? Well, I got an email today from the producers. They want us to compete in two weeks!"

"Are you serious?" Sadie gasped. "We're going to be on TV?"

They both jumped up and down and screamed.

"I am calling an emergency meeting of PLC tomorrow after school," Kylie said breathlessly. "We need a serious battle plan—and more hands on deck. I'm thinking we should call my camp friend Delaney and get her on board, too. And we'll need to watch every episode from the past three years and take notes."

Sadie's head was spinning, and things got even crazier as soon as Lexi and Jenna heard the news. They came to the teachers' lounge kitchen the next day with a long list of what the club needed for battle.

"Let's start with a dozen more tips for piping," Lexi said. "If we want to look like professionals, we need the right tools."

"And I wrote down key ingredients we have to bring," Jenna said. "Ten types of chocolate, three types of vanilla, some imported spices…"

"Whoa, guys, slow down!" Juliette said. "I think it's fine to create a wish list, but you have to be smart about this. You don't have an unlimited budget."

"But how will we win if we don't have all this?" Lexi insisted. "Those other bakers will be much more prepared."

"You'll do the best with what you have," Juliette replied. "You always have, and your cupcakes are amazing. This isn't a contest about who has more money to spend. It's about being creative and smart."

Kylie sighed. "In other words, we don't stand a chance. We're totally out of our league."

"If the producers thought that, they never would have asked you to compete," Juliette pointed out.

"Maybe they thought we'd provide some comic relief on the show," Jenna said. "We did leave in the part where Sadie got a flour shower."

"They obviously saw star quality in your club," Juliette said. "So let's just be optimistic, and you girls do what you do best: bake cupcakes!"

☆ ☮ ☆

Kylie thought it would be most efficient to divide and conquer, so she gave each of the girls an assignment. Lexi packed boxes with fondant, modeling chocolate, molds and assorted sprinkles, sanding sugars, and edible glitter. That way, they'd have tons of options for decorating, no matter what the challenge. Jenna was entrusted with all of PLC's recipes. She organized them by theme, flavor, and filling, and printed them out on recipe cards.

Sadie, Kylie, and Delaney divided the sixty-six previously aired episodes of *Battle of the Bakers* between them and took notes on what the judges liked or disliked and what the winners baked. Every episode consisted of two mystery challenges and ingredients—plus a final presentation round for the finalists. The last bakers standing were the winners.

"I'm definitely seeing a pattern," Sadie reported to her clubmates. "The judges hate when you use anything artificial like food coloring. This one baker won with a red velvet cupcake she made with beet juice."

"Eww, gross!" Jenna cried. "No beets are going near *my* cupcakes."

"Then there was this other guy who made a kale cupcake…" Sadie explained.

"Kale?" Delaney made a face. "As in that green stuff?"

"Yup," replied Sadie. "Topped with cream cheese frosting and crushed hazelnuts. The judges said it was 'divine.'"

"Beets, kale…doesn't anyone do a plain, old chocolate cupcake anymore?" Jenna sighed. "Has the entire world gone *loco*?"

"I think it would be fun for you to expand our horizons a little," Juliette suggested. "Beets or no beets, you should get a little creative."

The cupcake club decided a little practice would be a good idea. "Pretend I'm the judge," Juliette instructed. "This is just like *Battle of the Bakers*, girls. I'm going to give you a category, and you'll have sixty minutes to create a cupcake that is both delicious and artistically pleasing."

"I can handle the artistically pleasing part," Lexi said.

"I wouldn't be so sure about that!" Juliette chuckled. "Your category is caveman cupcakes, and your time starts now!"

The girls looked at each other, completely stumped.

"Did cavemen even *eat* cupcakes?" Sadie asked.

"Do you mean real cavemen...or like *The Flintstones*?" Jenna asked.

"Up to you! Any theme could come up on *Battle of the Bakers*," Juliette insisted. "Think outside the box!"

Kylie closed her eyes and tried to picture a prehistoric setting. "I'm thinking swamp beast..." she said.

"Ooh, swamp beast cupcakes. Yum!" Jenna said sarcastically.

"What about mud? Like the Mississippi mud pie cupcakes we once baked?" Sadie suggested.

"Exactly!" said Juliette. "Think about what you've perfected already and how you can adapt it to the theme!"

"We could add marshmallow rocks on top, and I could do different dinos out of chocolate, like a stegosaurus and a T. rex!" Lexi chimed in.

"What about cave paintings? It's a caveman cupcake... let's do some cave paintings on a chocolate cave. We can mold the cave shape by pouring milk chocolate into a funnel!" Jenna added.

"Brilliant, ladies! Get to it!" Juliette called. "You have fifty minutes left!"

They raced around the kitchen, tripping over each

other and spilling batter and chocolate everywhere. When the cupcakes came out of the oven, the cake was rich and gooey, and Jenna piped an extra large mound of chocolate marshmallow frosting on top. In the end, they presented three different cupcakes to Juliette on a platter—each one delicious and elaborately decorated.

"By George, I think you've got it!" Juliette cheered. "You could actually win this, girls!"

"Good thing we didn't make a *Tyrannosaurus wreck*," Jenna joked.

The girls groaned but felt revved and ready for battle!

The Battle Begins!

The night before the *Battle of the Bakers*, Sadie couldn't sleep a wink. She sat on the edge of her bed, dribbling her basketball and trying to go over all the things Juliette told them to remember: stay focused, double-check each measurement before you put in an ingredient, taste everything before you serve it to the judges. It was a lot like cramming for her math test. She knew she had to keep her cool and not panic, even if the clock was ticking down and they had thirty seconds left to finish the round.

When her alarm finally went off at 6 a.m., she grabbed her skateboard, raced downstairs, and waited anxiously at the door for Juliette's car to pick her up and take her to the TV studio. The rest of the audience—including Sadie's parents—would be in the studio for the taping at 10 a.m.

"She's not going to be here for an hour, hon," her mom said, yawning. "You want some breakfast?"

"I can't eat—I'm way too nervous!" Sadie said. "This is huge, Mom. Really huge. This can make or break a cupcake business!"

"I know, Sadie, but I want you to keep things in perspective. It's just a baking contest. It's not the end of the world if you guys don't win. You know that from basketball. It's not whether you win or lose, but how you play the game."

Sadie knew her mom was right, but this felt so much more important than any basketball game she had ever competed in. Maybe it was because PLC was something she had worked so hard to build from the ground up. This was the biggest and best thing that had ever happened to their cupcake club. They just *had* to win!

Juliette pulled up to Sadie's house fifteen minutes early. Kylie was already in the backseat and yanked Sadie in next to her. "Get in! Hurry! We have three more stops to make, and I want to be there super early!"

Sadie was happy to see that her BFF was as much a basket case as she was. "I couldn't sleep," Sadie confided.

"Me neither. I was up counting cupcake wrappers. I wanted to make sure we had enough for all the rounds— just in case we make it to the 500 cupcake finale!"

"Didn't I tell you guys to get some rest?" Juliette sighed. "You're going to fall asleep over your batter."

"Not a chance," Kylie assured her. "I'm not sleeping through PLC's TV debut!"

They picked up Lexi, Jenna, and Delaney and headed on the highway to the show's Westport studios. As soon as they entered the on-ramp, they were in bumper-to-bumper traffic.

"We're never going to get there!" Kylie whined. "Maybe try the right lane…or get off at the next exit and go on local streets?"

"No backseat drivers," Juliette replied. "We'll get there in plenty of time, I promise."

She kept her word: they arrived before any of the other contestants and had time to look around.

"You must be Peace, Love, and Cupcakes." A man wearing a headset rushed over to them. "I'm Jules Goldberg, associate producer."

"What gave us away?" Jenna joked, pointing to their PLC T-shirts.

"Yes, the shirts." Mr. Goldberg nodded. "But I also recognized you from your audition video. Very impressive!"

"We try!" Kylie smiled. "Are we the first bakers here?"

"Oh, yes. I don't expect the others to arrive for a while. This is old hat to them. They pretty much just show up for the taping."

Lexi gulped. "Old hat? You mean all of our competitors have already been on the show?"

"Yes," the producer said, checking his clipboard. "Or on other baking competitions. Or in national championships. We have quite a few champions in the house."

Sadie looked anxiously at Kylie. "Champions? They're putting us up against champions?"

"Relax, girls," Juliette assured them. "You're very well-prepared for *Battle of the Bakers*."

"I'm not so sure about that," Lexi said, picking up a strange plastic tool off a countertop. "I don't even know what this is."

"Um, I believe that is an icing comb," Juliette offered. "You use it for making ridges and swirls on cakes."

"Or for fixing your hair," Delaney said, pretending to touch up her blond ponytail. "Do I look ready for my close-up?"

"Have you ever *seen* a kitchen like this?" Sadie gasped. She glided around the floor on her skateboard. "It's huge! There are like six ovens and four fridges! I'm going to need my skateboard just to get from one end to the other!"

"What do you suppose this does?" Kylie said, picking up a strange tubelike object with a trigger. She pressed a button and a blue flame shot out.

"It's a blowtorch," Juliette said, grabbing it out of her hands. "You use it for desserts like crème brûlée. Do not touch! We don't want to set the place on fire before we even start baking."

Sadie was zipping from corner to corner, checking out the equipment. "And, Sadie, no skateboard," Juliette added. "I'm not sure the judges will appreciate cupcakes on wheels."

"Go on, ladies, get acquainted with your space. Set up your tools," Mr. Goldberg called over his shoulder. "You have plenty of time. I, on the other hand, have camera angles to check."

Three hours flew by as the girls made notes of everything that was in the pantry and tried to figure out how to start the timer on the industrial oven.

"Are you sure it will ring at twenty-two minutes? We don't want our cupcakes to burn!" Kylie said, watching Sadie punch the numbers on the digital panel.

"Kylie, we've practiced a dozen times. It works just fine," Sadie insisted.

"This is just so different from our kitchens at home,"

Kylie added. "It's all so big and modern. I'm used to my mom's old KitchenAid—not this high-tech blender-mixer-thingamajig."

"They really do have everything a baker could want," Juliette said. "It's amazing. You girls should be very excited to have all of this at your fingertips."

"I have never seen so many piping tips." Lexi's eyes were wide. "I think I've died and gone to cupcake heaven."

"That's the spirit," Juliette said. "Think of the possibilities!"

Just then, a noisy group entered the studio.

"OMG!" cried Sadie. "That's him! That's Benny Volero, the Cake King! That guy's won every Food Network competition he's ever been on. He's a pro! He built a replica of the *Titanic* out of cake and sank it in a swimming pool!"

Lexi nodded. "He's a legend. Seriously, how can we ever expect to win against him?"

Sadie glanced across the kitchen set. Benny was signing autographs for the cameramen. He had two commercial mixers, a fondant roller machine, and his own personal piping tips—not to mention a team of six guys in white chef coats. Her stomach did a flip-flop.

"Didn't anyone tell him the kitchen is fully stocked?" Delaney wondered out loud.

"He's Benny. He's the best of the best—so he needs the best stuff," Kylie explained.

"He's not so tough," Jenna piped up. "What's he got that we don't?"

"A hit TV show, a chain of bakeries, about a dozen cookbooks with his name on them..." Sadie sighed. "I think he even has a street named after him in Stamford."

"Oh," Jenna winced. "Good point."

"But what we lack in experience, we make up for in style!" Kylie tried to cheer on her team.

"That's right," Juliette insisted. "You girls have come a long way, and you're going to give these bakers a good fight."

The girls watched as the rest of the bakers filed in. The next ones to arrive were the Connecticut Cupcake sisters, Cece and Chloe.

"They are so organized," Sadie whispered. "Look at all those ingredients in perfect little pink jars and boxes. They even have pink bows in their hair to match!"

Then there was Dina Pinkerton, Sugar Fingers owner and a two-time *Battle of the Bakers* winner.

"Oh, no...not her!" Kylie pretended to bang her head against the kitchen counter.

"The judges love her…we're doomed," said Jenna. "She's a whiz with vegan cupcakes. You can't top her tofu frosting, trust me."

Sadie had to admit the competition looked pretty fierce. How could a group of fifth-graders stand a chance? Then she remembered a basketball game she'd played two years earlier against Rye Country Day School.

"You never know! Sometimes, at the last minute, someone steals the ball," she told her cupcake club.

"There are no basketballs here, Sadie," Kylie reminded her. "Just cupcakes."

"And your skateboard." Jenna giggled.

"My point is I was once up against this *giant* girl from Rye Country Day School," Sadie continued. "She was nine years old and about six feet tall! Everyone thought she was unbeatable. Well, I stole the ball right out from between her hands and I won the game. We creamed those Rye Reptiles!"

"So you're saying there is someone who is actually *taller* than you in elementary school?" Jenna asked. "I don't believe it."

"I think what Sadie is trying to say is 'nothing is impossible,'" Kylie stepped in. "Am I right?"

Sadie smiled. "I knew you'd get it. And I swear, this girl was at least a head taller than me!"

☆ ☮ ☆

Jerry Wolcott, host of *Battle of the Bakers*, suddenly summoned everyone to attention. "That's my cue to go to my seat in the audience," Juliette said. "Break an egg, girls. Make me proud!"

There was no more time for nerves or self-doubt. "Cupcake bakers, may I please have one representative from each team in the center of the kitchen?" Jerry called. "This person will be the team captain."

Benny strolled over, looking confident. And Cece stepped forward (after she and Chloe thumb-wrestled for it). Kylie looked at Sadie. "You go," she said. "Sadie, you're a real competitor—you know what it takes to win. You never give up."

Sadie gulped. "Me? But Kylie, you're the club president. You should be the leader. Besides, what if they give us something to read? What about my dyslexia?"

Jenna gave her a little push. "Come on, *chica*, you can do it. Put on your game face and get out there!"

Lexi gave her hand a squeeze. "We believe in you, Sadie."

Sadie walked slowly to the middle of the room where three other bakers were gathered, awaiting instructions as the camera crew tested the spotlights. She stood next to Dina Pinkerton, who was adjusting her apron. She looked cool as a cucumber. Sadie nibbled her nails.

"Hey." Dina smiled. "I've heard some great things about your cupcakes."

Sadie smiled back timidly. "Thanks."

"You nervous?" Dina asked.

Sadie thought about what her basketball coach had told her a million times: "Don't let the other team see you sweat. Put on your best game face."

"Um, no, not at all," she lied. "I'm cool." She wasn't sure who she was trying to convince, Dina or herself.

"Good!" Dina replied. "Because I'm a wreck! I am before every competition. But adrenaline is a good thing, you know?"

"It is?"

"Sure! Just try to focus on taste, texture, and presentation, and keep an eye on the clock. And whatever you do, don't put maraschino cherries on your cupcakes."

"Why?" Sadie asked, puzzled.

"Because the head judge, Fiero Boulangerie, *hates* them. You'll lose if you do—trust me!"

Sadie smiled. "Thanks for the tip!"

"I've got another tip for you," whispered Benny. "Make sure your cupcakes have some zip and zing…if you know what I mean."

Sadie scratched her head. "Um, no, I don't know what you mean."

"A little extra excitement—something that takes it over the top," Benny explained.

"Oh!" said Sadie. "Like the time you made a Fourth of July cupcake on *The Cake King* show and it exploded?"

Cece rolled her eyes. "You don't have to throw in all those splashy tricks," she advised. "Just make sure your cupcakes are moist and you use the best quality ingredients. That's how we've become a success."

Sadie tried to take it all in: zip and zing, no cherries, best ingredients. She thought her head was going to explode like Benny's Fourth of July cupcake!

"Places! Places, everyone!" Jerry summoned them. "No more talking. I'd like to introduce you to the judges and then we'll start filming."

Sadie stared out at the audience—it was a packed room. Everyone was watching! Her mom and dad were in the front row, waving at her. Please, Sadie thought, don't let them fight!

Three people walked onto the kitchen set: Fiero, Carly Nielson, owner of Jimmies, the world's first cupcakery, and…

Sadie gasped. No! It couldn't be!

"I'm sure you know *Battle of the Bakers*' two famous judges, Fiero and Carly," Jerry said. "And our guest judge today is Mrs. Lila Vanderwall, president of the New Fairfield Art Society."

Sadie glanced over her shoulder at her fellow PLC members, who looked as shocked and sick to their stomachs as she felt.

"What's wrong?" Delaney whispered.

"Big *problema*!" Jenna gulped. "Mrs. Vanderwall hates Peace, Love, and Cupcakes! We messed up her order."

"'Messed up' is putting it mildly," Kylie added. "We almost caused an epic art society fail."

"Well, maybe Mrs. Vanderwall has forgotten," Delaney offered. "I'm sure it's all bygones."

Just then, a shriek arose from the judging table: "You! I know you!" Mrs. Vanderwall was pointing an accusing finger at Sadie. "You almost destroyed my event!"

Sadie tried to keep her guard up. "It was an accident," she said softly. "Nice to see you again, Mrs. Vanderwall."

The other bakers looked stunned. They'd never seen a judge get this angry *before* she tasted a single cupcake.

Jerry tried to calm her down by doing a magic trick: he pulled a quarter out of her ear. "Hey, Mrs. V—look at that! *Ears* to you!" Fiero and Carly chuckled.

But Mrs. Vanderwall was not amused. "I do not like magic tricks," she sniffed. "I do not like puns, and I do not like bakers who are unprofessional." She settled into her seat and continued glaring at Sadie.

"Okay…someone needs a little sugar to sweeten her attitude!" Jerry joked. "So let's give it to her. Bakers, here is your first challenge. The first round requires you to make a cupcake that will wow our judges." He pointed to the table piled high with ingredients. "But here's the fun part: you must use two ingredients, one from Section A, one from Section B, that don't go together. This challenge is called The Perfect Pair."

Sadie stared at the table: in Section A, there were tons of snack foods, stuff like potato chips, popcorn, peanut butter, granola, and a mountain of jelly beans. In section B, there were fruits, veggies, hot peppers, and even a jar of pickles.

"Holy cannoli!" Benny cried, mopping his brow. "What are we supposed to do with that?"

"That's for you to bake and us to partake!" Jerry danced around. He pointed to the giant digital clock on the back wall of the studio. "And your time starts *now*!"

Sadie raced back to her team. "What do we want from the table? What can we bake?"

"It's all so yucky," Jenna said. "None of those things go together!"

"Think out of the box, you guys," Kylie pleaded. "There has to be something!"

"What if we do a chocolate potato chip cupcake?" asked Delaney.

"Way too safe," said Lexi. "This is *Battle of the Bakers*. They want creativity. They want to see something that's never been done before. I've watched every episode. Trust me—we need to take a big risk."

"How about popcorn and papaya? Or pickles and Pop-Tarts?" Kylie suggested.

"Eww, eww, and eww!" Jenna insisted. "This has to be yummy or we're heading home in Round 1."

Sadie was the only one not tossing out suggestions. She was too busy looking at the ingredients table, her mind racing a million miles a minute.

"Guys," she said softly. "I think I know what to make."

The girls stopped bickering. "What?" Kylie asked. "Tell us! We only have fifty-five minutes left!"

"My parents are the perfect pair—even though they argue all the time. They belong together."

"We know you're worried about your folks getting divorced," Jenna said. "But what does this have to do with cupcakes?"

"Let's do the two foods my parents like combined in a cupcake. That way we won't just win Round 1, but maybe they'll see what a perfect pair *they* are and won't break up."

The girls were all quiet. "It's a great idea, Sadie," Kylie said, putting her arm around her friend. "But what are their two favorite foods?"

"That's the tricky part," Sadie said. "They really don't go together—but I think we can pull it off." She whispered in Kylie's ear.

"Oh, no. Really?" Kylie sighed. "Okay, let's put it to a quick vote: all in favor of a chili and cheesecake cupcake, raise your hand."

Jenna gasped. "Chili and cheesecake? *Un momento, por favor!* How spicy are we talking?"

"Hot. My dad likes his chili very, very hot. Like three-alarm-blaze hot."

"Ouch!" said Delaney. "We want to wow the judges… not set them on fire."

"I think we can do it," Kylie interrupted. "A sweet, light, cream cheese frosting would balance out the heat of the cupcake."

Jenna nodded. "We could blend some chili spices into a dark chocolate batter. My *abuela* made a delicious 'hot chocolate' cake once. I think I remember how…some cayenne, a little ground chili pepper…"

"And I can make a realistic chili pepper out of fondant and put it on top of the cupcake," Lexi offered.

Sadie cheered. "I knew we could pull it off!"

"Not so fast," Kylie reminded them. "We haven't pulled it off yet. And the clock is down to forty-five minutes."

"Cupcake bakers, opposites attract…but will you repel the judges?" Jerry teased. "Forty-five minutes left!"

"Team PLC," Sadie said, pulling them all into a huddle, just like she'd seen her coach do. "Two-four-six-eight, let's get baking something great!"

Up in the Air

As the cupcake club scrambled to figure out their recipe, the rest of the bakers in the battle were also struggling.

"I said I wanted fresh mozzarella," Benny shouted, throwing shredded cheese at one of his assistants as the cameraman zoomed in for a close-up. "How many times do I have to tell you?"

"Is he making a pizza or a cupcake?" Jenna asked.

"And those sisters do nothing but fight!" Lexi pointed out.

Cece and Chloe were having a tug-of-war in the middle of their kitchen as Mr. Goldberg, the associate producer, instructed the sound technicians to make sure they were catching every word.

"I'm making the frosting," Cece yelled, grabbing a pink bowl out of Chloe's hands. "Mommy says I make the best frosting!"

"Mommy always likes your cupcakes better than mine!" whined Chloe. "But this time I'm doing the frosting!"

"OMG, did you say these people were *professionals*?" Delaney asked. "They sound more like little kids in the school yard!"

"It doesn't matter what everyone else is doing," Kylie said, trying to focus her team. Then she spotted Dina whipping up her signature tofu frosting...and pouring in pickle juice! "Did you guys see that? What is she doing?"

Sadie stepped in and took charge. "Guys, Kylie's right. We have to concentrate on our cupcake!"

"We want this dark chocolate cupcake to have some fire to it," Jenna said. She carefully measured one-eighth of a teaspoon of cayenne pepper and gently mixed it into the batter. "This should do it."

"Are you sure?" Kylie asked. "I mean, are you positive it's not going to set the judges mouths on fire?"

"Remember what Benny told me," Sadie cautioned. "It has to have a little zip and zing...or was it zing and zip? I can't remember!"

"I tasted it three times...it's great," Jenna insisted.

"But does it need to be hotter?" Lexi chimed in. "Sometimes the judges complain they can't taste the heat."

Jenna stepped back from the bowl. "A little faith, please?" she said. "I am the official PLC taster, *sí*?"

"Jenna's right," Kylie said. "We have to get these cupcakes into the oven. We can't second-guess everything."

"Maybe just a pinch more cinnamon?" Sadie pleaded. "My dad's chili is *really* spicy."

Jenna nodded, sprinkled in a pinch more cinnamon, a dash more cayenne, and took a final taste. "*Vámanos!*" she said. "To the oven!"

While they waited for the cupcakes to bake, Lexi and Delaney sculpted tiny fondant chili peppers, and Kylie and Sadie mixed the cinnamon cream-cheese frosting.

"Do we want creamy or whippy?" Kylie pondered, turning on the mixer.

"Definitely whippy," Jenna called. "The lighter and airier, the more it will balance out the richness of the cake."

"Fiero always likes it when frosting melts on his tongue," Sadie recalled. "He said so in at least six episodes."

"Whippy it is!" said Kylie, cranking the mixer to its highest setting.

☆ ☮ ☆

"Bakers…twenty minutes is all you've got! Will your cupcakes be cool or not so hot?" Jerry called.

"Okay, now that guy is getting on my nerves!" Jenna exclaimed. She stood at the oven door, watching the cupcakes rise. "They have to be the perfect, spongy, moist consistency. Not too dense…not too gooshy."

"What's 'gooshy'?" Delaney asked. "Is that a baking term?"

"It's a Jenna term," Sadie explained. "It means the cake is too lumpy and uncooked in the center."

"I think 'gooshy' sounds better," Jenna insisted. She opened the oven door and stuck a toothpick in the center of a cupcake. When it came out clean, she announced, "*Perfecto!*" and headed for the freezer to cool them down in a flash.

"Ten minutes!" Jerry's voice rang through the studio.

Kylie started to panic. "Oh, no! We need to get them frosted *now*!"

"Keep calm, girls!" Juliette called from the audience.

Lexi had her pastry bag loaded and ready to fire. "Bring 'em out!" she called.

"A few more minutes! They're not cool enough!" Jenna shouted.

"We don't have a few more minutes!" Sadie pleaded. "We need them *now*! Hurry!"

Jenna raced with the baking tray toward the counter. But just as she was about to place the cupcakes down, she stepped on Sadie's skateboard and went sprawling backward. The cupcakes flew out of the tray and into the air.

"Oh, no!" screamed Kylie. "They're going to fall on the floor!"

"I got it! I got it!" Sadie screamed, jumping as high as she could and grabbing two cupcakes in each hand.

"Put them on the plate!" Lexi shouted, as the rest of the cupcakes—and Jenna—landed with a *splat* on the kitchen tiles. Sadie set the cupcakes in front of Lexi, who perfectly swirled the frosting on each of them, sprinkled them with cinnamon, and topped them off with the fondant chili peppers.

"Time's up! Step away from your cupcakes!" Jerry called.

The girls stepped away from the counter, panting and sweating.

"Yow!" yelped Jenna. "Don't step on me! Girl on the floor, remember?"

"That was close…too close!" Sadie tried to catch her breath. She helped Jenna to her feet. "You okay?"

"Lucky for me I had some nice soft cupcakes to break

my fall," Jenna joked. She was covered in dark chocolate cupcake crumbs. "Pretty tasty, if I do say so myself!"

"Ladies and gentleman," Jerry called. "Please present your cupcakes to the judges!"

PLC was up first. "What do I say?" Sadie shook Kylie by the shoulders. "I don't know what to say!"

"Just say what you told us. Explain why this cupcake is The Perfect Pair, just like your parents."

Sadie took a deep breath and approached the judges' table. She knew her parents and her brothers, not to mention everyone at Blakely Elementary, would be home watching them on live TV. Mrs. Vanderwall's lips were tightly pursed, as if she was ready to take a bite out of both Sadie and the cupcake.

"This cupcake is The Perfect Pair because it's inspired by two people who belong together," she said into the camera. "My parents, Bria and Gabriel Harris."

"That's so sweet!" Carly cooed. "Tell us more, Sadie."

"Well, my mom and dad are really opposites. He likes hip-hop music and she likes opera. He watches sports and she loves old romantic movies. Sometimes they fight because they don't see eye to eye, but I know that deep down, they really love each other. This cupcake combines two of their favorite foods that don't really sound like they would go together: spicy chili and cheesecake. But when you combine them in a cupcake…well, they're the perfect pair. Just like my parents."

Sadie held her breath, stared straight ahead, and braced herself for the judges' critiques.

"Zees coopcake…it eez rich…it eez moist…it eez *magnifique!*" Fiero said.

"Did he just say he liked it? I can't understand his French accent!" Delaney whispered.

Carly nodded. "I think the hot chocolaty cake and the light cheese frosting blend together beautifully. I was licking my plate. It was yummy."

Finally, Mrs. Vanderwall raised her fork and took a bite. "Hmmmm…" she mumbled. "Mmmm…..mmmmm…. mmmmm!"

Sadie looked puzzled—was that an "I like it" or an "I hate it"?

"Do you have something to add, Mrs. V?" Jerry asked.

"From an artistic standpoint, the decoration was quite realistic."

Lexi jumped up and down. "Yes! She liked my pepper!"

"But the flavor…it's a *mistake*." She said the last word so loudly that Sadie flinched.

"She will never get over it," Kylie cried. "She's not going to even give us a chance!"

"Why is it a mistake?" Jerry asked.

"I simply don't appreciate spiciness and creaminess together," Mrs. Vanderwall replied. "That's my opinion."

When it was the other contestants' turns, the judges were also divided.

"I think your pickle and parsnip cupcake is clever," Carly told Dina. "But I'm missing some sweetness. I wanted more of a treat."

"Your marinara and marshmallow coopcake…it was a miss for me," Fiero told Benny. "You go too far out of zee box."

Mrs. Vanderwall commended Cece and Chloe for their Pretty in Pink cupcake. "I love the way you created a cloud of cotton candy over the red beet buttercream," she cooed. "Such brilliant use of color."

"Beets," Jenna fumed. "I hate beets!"

But Fiero pointed out that the frosting overpowered their rose-petal-infused cake. "I cannot taste zee flowers," he complained. "Where are zay? Did zay disappear?"

Sadie went back to her team. "I think it's anyone's game," she said. "I'm not sure who will go home first."

"I hope it's not us," said Lexi. "That would be really embarrassing!"

"You did an awesome job presenting, Sadie," Kylie said. "You did your best."

"I hope my parents liked it," she replied. "Do you think they did?"

Kylie shrugged. "They left right after the judging."

"They left?" Sadie gasped. "Why? Are they mad at me?"

"I'm not sure," Kylie said, trying to calm her. "I'm sure it's nothing. Maybe your dad had a work emergency. Or your brother Ty set fire to the toaster again. They just probably had to go and didn't want to distract you."

Sadie hated feeling helpless. She wished she could go back and redo the entire first round—rewind the morning in instant replay mode and change everything. She had probably upset her parents and they were mad or embarrassed. But the judges were already huddled at their table, deciding who would stay and who would go.

"Bakers, please face the judges," Jerry commanded.

"No matter what happens, we're right behind you," Kylie said, patting Sadie on the back.

Jerry held a card in his hands. "I have here the results of Round 1," he began. "One of you is cake royalty…but you failed to make a cupcake that could wow our judges. Benny…I'm sorry. You're done at *Battle of the Bakers*."

Benny's eyes grew wide. "But I'm the Cake King…"

"Yes, yes you are." Jerry shook his hand. "But for now… it's *ciao*!"

"I don't believe it!" Kylie exclaimed. "We made Round 2!"

"It was totally my skateboard wipeout that did it…I'm great on TV," Jenna teased.

"Whatever it was, we really have to bring it in the next round!" said Kylie.

Their cheering section went wild: Kylie's mom and dad waved a big poster that read, "Peace, Love, and Cupcakes is sweet!" and Lexi's big sister, Ava, high-fived Jenna's big sis Gabriella.

"Go, PLC!" Juliette shouted from the audience. Her boyfriend, Mr. Higgins, was also there, giving them a thumbs-up.

"Look! Jeremy came!" Lexi said. "That is sooooo nice!" He and his parents waved from the third row and were seated with Delaney's mom and dad.

Sadie combed the audience for her parents, but there was no sign of them. She didn't have much time to worry, though. Jerry summoned her back to the stage for the next round's instructions. And like Coach always told her, she needed to get her head in the game.

"This round calls for the opposite of your Round 1 creation. For this baking battle, turn your cupcakes upside down. You have ninety minutes! Go!"

Sadie raced back to the kitchen. "I don't get it. Is that some kind of riddle?"

"I don't know," said Kylie. "They've never done this on *Battle of the Bakers* before!"

"Wait, maybe Jenna can fall again and the cupcakes will land upside down on the judges' laps?" Delaney suggested.

"Maybe Jerry means we should reverse what we did with the first cupcake?" Sadie questioned. "Like instead of a hot chocolate cake, make a cold one…"

"And instead of cool frosting, make it hot?" Kylie followed her train of thought.

Jenna shook her head. "No way…it can't be done! In ninety minutes? Not a chance!"

"What? What can't be done?" Delaney asked anxiously.

Sadie shrugged. "It's worth a try. If we pull it off, we'll be the first team to ever do a hot fudge sundae cupcake on *Battle of the Bakers*!"

Cupcakes à la Mode

"Go through that pantry and find us some ice cream!" Sadie said, shoving Delaney toward the freezer.

"We'll need to melt Belgian chocolate on the stove slowly," said Jenna. "It has to pour smooth and thick over the top of the cupcake."

"The ice-cream scoop needs to sit on a cupcake," Kylie added. "What's the best flavor we make?"

"Vanilla bean!" the girls shouted in unison.

"Then vanilla bean it is! Let's get baking!"

Sadie knew the recipe by heart: 2 ¼ cups of flour, 1 ½ cups of sugar, 1 tablespoon baking powder, 1 teaspoon salt, 1 cup of whole milk, 4 eggs, 1 stick of butter, 2 teaspoons pure vanilla extract, and of course, the seeds from one vanilla bean.

"See, you're pretty good with memorizing numbers," Kylie told her. "Ms. Erikka would be proud!"

While the cupcake base baked, Delaney and Jenna worked at the stove, creating the perfect hot fudge sauce. In a pan, they mixed condensed milk, semi-sweet chocolate, and two tablespoons of butter until the mixture took on a smooth, glossy texture.

Once the cupcakes cooled, Sadie placed a scoop of vanilla ice cream on top, and Lexi drizzled the chocolate over it, making a delicate web. "Should we put a cherry on top?" Delaney asked.

"No cherries! No cherries!" Sadie shouted. "Fiero hates cherries." A cameraman shoved a camera in her face, trying to catch her in a moment of panic.

"Yes, thank you, we've got it all under control." Kylie smiled and waved into the lens. Then she whispered to Sadie, "We can't freak out on TV. These cameras are recording everything we do and say."

Instead of cherries, Lexi made a white chocolate peace sign and perched it on top of the fudge and ice cream.

They had only seconds remaining before Jerry called time. "PLC...you presented first last time, so this time you'll be last."

"Oh, no!" Sadie panicked. "The ice cream will melt!"

"Let's hope the other bakers talk really fast," Kylie said,

crossing her fingers. "Or we're going to be serving the judges hot fudge soup!"

Cece and Chloe went first. "Since Carly said our last cupcake needed to be more of a treat, we filled this one with candy!" Cece explained.

Fiero took a bite. "What is zees? I think I cracked my tooth on it!" he cried.

"Oh, that's a gum ball," Cece replied.

"It is like a rock. Zees is bad. Very bad!" he grumbled.

Dina's cupcake was exactly what Jerry asked for: upside down. "I put the frosting in the wrapper, then placed the cake on top," she grinned. "Like a little hat! I call it Topsy Turvy."

"Well, you definitely kept to the theme," Carly said. "But I don't think you gave us anything fresh or new from the last round. I wanted to taste something different. I'm a little over the pickles and parsnips. You didn't work very hard to impress us."

Finally, it was Sadie's turn.

"Well, we decided to make our cupcake the opposite of our first one. The cake is cold—it's ice cream—and the topping is hot—it's fudge."

Fiero looked down at his plate. "And zees? What is zees white thing on top?"

"Oh, that was supposed to be a white chocolate peace sign—for Peace, Love, and Cupcakes," Sadie answered. "I guess it melted."

"My coopcake…it eez soggy. I like the cake part, but the ice cream, it eez how you say…"

"Gooshy!" Jenna shouted from the wings. "I call it gooshy!"

"*Oui*, like the girl says. It eez gooshy!"

Carly put down her fork and used a spoon to taste it. "I have to agree with Fiero. I like the flavor of your vanilla bean cupcake, and the chocolate fudge is divine, but the ice cream made this sad little puddle on my plate."

"Oh, no," Kylie groaned. "She thinks our cupcake is sad!"

As if that wasn't bad enough, Mrs. Vanderwall threw in, "Yes, very disappointing indeed!"

While the judges deliberated, the cupcake club members huddled in their kitchen.

"Don't give up yet," Sadie begged. "Fiero chipped a tooth…maybe they'll be disqualified for that."

☆ ☮ ☆

Jerry cleared his throat. "Okay, bakers, time to face the judges."

Sadie took her spot in between Cece and Dina.

"This was not an easy decision," Carly began. "We didn't feel that any of the bakers truly baked cupcakes worthy of *Battle of the Bakers* in this round."

Sadie's heart was doing jumping jacks. Had they all failed? Were they *all* going home?

"However, one baker did nothing new to impress us with her cupcake," Carly continued. "Dina…I'm sorry, you're done in *Battle of the Bakers*."

"That's okay…I've won twice. Time to pass the torch!" Dina said. Then she winked at Sadie. "Good luck!"

Rock and Roll

Sadie had no time to let the good news sink in before Jerry started barking orders.

"Cupcake bakers! You have two hours to create a 500-cupcake display. Since you've spent all day learning that opposites attract, we want to see a cupcake display that proves it. You can use a master builder of your own and one additional assistant. Ready...set...bake!"

"We want Mommy to help us!" Cece and Chloe yelled. Their mother appeared from the side of the set, giving them a thumbs-up. "And my husband, Stan, the NASA engineer," Cece said, grinning.

"What do you think Connecticut Cupcake is going to make?" Lexi asked.

"We can't worry about them," Kylie insisted. "Our display has to stand on its own two feet."

"That's it!" Sadie yelled. "Two feet!" She grabbed a

pencil and made a stick figure. Then she drew another on the other side of the page.

"What is that supposed to be?" Lexi said, turning Sadie's drawing upside down. "It looks like a bunny rabbit...or maybe a turtle with a top hat?"

"It's not a bunny or a turtle," Sadie explained. "See? It's a couple?"

"A couple of what?" teased Jenna.

"A man and a woman," Sadie sighed. "You guys...it'll work! Trust me!"

Kylie looked over Sadie's scribbles. "I get it. What if we put them on wheels and push them together? Each one will have his and her own cupcakes, and then in the middle, we'll mix the two together. See...opposites attract."

"And let's make the frosting two different flavors, for example, sweet chocolate and salty peanut butter, so when they come together, they make a beautiful new swirled frosting," said Lexi.

Sadie was relieved that PLC had a game plan, but she was still worried what Cece and Chloe were up to. She looked over and saw their sketch: it was a giant "U" shape covered with mini-cupcakes coated in silver fondant.

"What are they making? A horseshoe?" Delaney asked.

Kylie shook her head. "Not a horseshoe. A giant magnet. It's really clever."

"But our idea is better," Sadie insisted. "If we can build it."

"Did someone say they needed a builder?" came a voice from the edge of the set.

"Daddy?" Sadie gasped. "What are you doing here? I thought you and Mom were mad at me."

"After that sweet presentation? Not a chance!" said Mrs. Harris. "Thank you, Sadie. It was really lovely. We were trying to get backstage to tell you."

Sadie smiled. "So you're not getting divorced?"

"Divorced? Where did you ever get such an idea?" Mr. Harris replied. "Sometimes parents fight when they're stressed, honey. It doesn't mean we're getting divorced."

"We're sorry if we upset you. We're going to try our very best to work things out…together." Mrs. Harris squeezed her husband's hand and smiled. "But for now, you girls have a cupcake battle to win!"

"Dad, can you be our master builder? And Mom, can you be our extra assistant?" Sadie asked. She handed her mother a purple PLC apron.

"We would love to!" her parents said, hugging her.

Sadie stretched out on a big sheet of plywood and lay down on it so Lexi could trace her outline. "You are way too tall!" Lexi laughed. "My hand is getting tired drawing you!"

"The plan is to cut two of these out and then Lexi will paint one to look like a man, the other to look like a woman," Kylie explained to Sadie's father. "Then we'll need to build some shelves so it looks like they're holding the cupcakes in their hands."

"Got it," said Mr. Harris. "And I can put them both on a rolling track so they come together with a light push."

"We still have 500 cupcakes to bake!" Sadie remembered. "And the clock is ticking down!"

"I got the chocolate…" said Jenna.

"I'm on the peanut butter," said Kylie.

"And we'll need a third group that's chocolate with peanut butter filling—I can do that!" said Delaney.

"Wait…Sadie, how many of each type of cupcake do we need?" Kylie asked. "What's the equation?"

Sadie bristled: "How should I know?" *Really?* Did Kylie have to throw math at her now, when they were all under so much pressure?

"Think, Sadie. You can do it. And we need to know how many of each flavor to bake."

Sadie pictured the 500 cupcakes divided into three groups. "Make 166 chocolate and 166 peanut butter. That's almost 14 dozen of each. Then let's do 168 chocolate and peanut butter swirl cupcakes. So 166 + 166 + 168 = 500."

Kylie grinned. "Awesome, Sadie. We're on it!"

By the time the first coat of paint had dried on their display, the cupcakes were coming out of the ovens.

"How are we doing on time?" asked Sadie. She had already piped five dozen chocolate cupcakes with chocolate fudge.

"Less than an hour left," Lexi sighed. "I'm getting nervous. We're so outnumbered!"

"Just keep painting and piping," said Mr. Harris. "I'll get this track working." But as much he pushed and pulled, the two figures refused to roll together.

"I think the weight of the large shelves is slowing them down," he explained. "We need bigger wheels."

Just then, Sadie had a brilliant idea. "Dad, what about my skateboard?"

"That might work," he said, unscrewing the wheels from the board and attaching them to the display. He gave a push and the two figures glided gracefully together in the center.

"Awesome!" Sadie cheered. "Now let's get those cupcakes on!"

The girls formed an assembly line, passing the cupcakes from Jenna and Lexi down to Delaney, Kylie, and finally Mrs. Harris and Sadie to put on the shelves. "Keep 'em coming. Keep 'em coming!" Sadie coached. "Faster! Faster!"

Jerry was pacing back and forth in front of the giant kitchen clock.

"Three minutes…two minutes…one minute left!" the host called. "Hurry!"

As a buzzer sounded, Sadie placed the last of the 500 cupcakes on the display.

"It's really amazing," Mr. Harris said. "A masterpiece if I ever saw one."

Sadie looked over at the Connecticut Cupcake display. *It* was amazing: a giant spinning magnet covered in metallic silver cupcakes. The top of it shot off sparks.

"Wow, that is really cool," Sadie said. "And hard to top. Let's hope the judges agree with you, Dad."

☆ ☮ ☆

When it was time to reveal the winner, Jerry had all the bakers gather in the center of the studio. "Connecticut

Cupcakes…Peace, Love, and Cupcakes, you both put up a valiant fight. One of you made a giant cupcake magnet that shoots fireworks; the other created a perfect pair that joined together with a chocolate-peanut butter kiss. In the end, only one can take home the prize. Only one can win *Battle of the Bakers*."

Sadie held her breath. Say our name! Say our name! she silently pleaded with him.

"Congratulations…Connecticut Cupcake!" Chloe, Cece, and their mommy jumped up and down, screaming and hugging one another.

Sadie felt like someone had sucked the air out of her… like when she ran over a nail with her bicycle tire. "We lost?" she said. "How could we lose?"

"You girls were amazing," Mr. Harris said. "You're champions in my eyes."

"That's really nice, Dad," said Sadie. "But we didn't win the $5,000. We didn't win the *Battle of the Bakers*."

"It's okay, Sadie." Kylie tried to comfort her. "We were still on TV—which means a lot of people saw PLC and will be ordering our cupcakes."

"Really? Would you want to order cupcakes from a losing team?" Jenna moped. "I don't know about you, but I'd be on the phone to Connecticut Cupcake ordering a dozen of those Pretty in Pinks."

Juliette ran up from the audience and gave them each a hug. "Good job, girls. You really looked and acted like pros out there. I am so, so proud of you all!"

☆ ☮ ☆

When Sadie got home, every muscle ached. She flopped down on her bed, not having the energy to even take off her frosting-stained apron and clothes.

"You look like you've been through a war," her brother Tyler remarked.

"Not a war. A battle. I can't move."

"I saw you on TV. The cupcake you did for Mom and Dad? That was pretty cool." It wasn't very often that her brother paid her a compliment.

Sadie smiled. "Thanks. I really want things to get better for our family."

"They will," Tyler said, patting her on the shoulder. "Money may be tight, but the Harrises put up a fight!"

"I'm glad you're getting A's in math," Sadie teased. "Because you are one awful poet!"

"Seriously, little sis, you know it's gonna be okay, right?"

Tyler gave her arm a playful punch. "Dad says we're just going through a rough patch. And you know he's really good at smoothing out rough patches with sandpaper."

Just then, Sadie remembered: the Golden Spoon roof!

"I almost forgot!" she said, jumping off her bed. She suddenly felt a second wind of energy—maybe her father had some good news. "Thanks for the pep talk!" She gave her brother a punch back.

"*Ow!* Take it easy! That hurt!" Tyler whined.

"Wimp!" Sadie giggled, and headed downstairs.

She found her father hunched over his desk, looking over blueprints.

"Hey, Dad…I could sure use some good news. How's the Golden Spoon coming?"

"Oh, it's coming…slowly and surely," he answered. "Mr. Ludwig likes to change his mind a lot, so I had to make some revisions. But I think you and your friends should put a week from Sunday on your calendar."

"What's that?" Sadie asked.

"The grand reopening of the Golden Spoon in Greenwich!"

The Icing on the Cake

Jenna thumbed through PLC's recipe file, searching for the perfect cupcake to bake for the Golden Spoon's grand reopening party.

"It should be something golden delicious," she said.

"Like the apple?" asked Delaney.

"No...like a golden cake. How 'bout this?" Jenna pushed a recipe card in front of Kylie.

"A lemonade cupcake? Well, it's definitely the right color..."

"How about pineapple? Or banana?" Delaney suggested.

Lexi shook her head. "We've done those tons of times. It's such a special occasion that we should do something really spectacular."

Sadie took a stack of recipe cards from Jenna and flipped through them. "No, no, no....*yes!*"

She pulled a card out and placed it on the table in front of her friends.

"Whoa…that looks awesome," Jenna said. "But we've never tried it like that before."

"How hard could it be?" Kylie pondered, skimming the ingredients. "It's a basic golden cake and caramel oozes out of the center…makes my mouth water just thinking about it!"

"I love the gold sugar crystals on the frosting," Lexi said. "Too bad we don't have one of those fondant printers like the Cake King had. We could do the Golden Spoon logo on top."

"All agreed…say 'cupcake'!" Kylie said.

"CUPCAKE!" everyone yelled, seconding the motion.

☆ ⊕ ☆

Six hours later, Sadie, Mrs. Harris, and the girls were helping her father load his truck with twelve dozen Golden Caramel cupcakes.

"You're gonna save me one, right?" Mr. Harris asked his daughter.

"Are you kidding? After all the hard work you did on the Golden Spoon? You can have two!" Sadie hugged him.

When they arrived in Greenwich, a big crowd was already lined up outside the door.

"Wow," Kylie remarked. "Looks like Mr. Ludwig's customers missed him!"

"Or they missed PLC's cupcakes," Mrs. Harris pointed out.

They piled out of the truck and knocked on the door. Mr. Ludwig was watching out the window with a huge smile on his face. "You're here! You're here! Please come in!"

Sadie had never seen him so excited. He practically skipped to the door to open it. He was dressed in a lavender suit with a metallic gold tie.

"Close your eyes," he insisted. "Don't look just yet!"

The girls obeyed as Mr. Ludwig guided them through the door and into the store.

"You, too!" Mr. Harris said, covering his wife's eyes. "No peeking!"

"I feel like I'm on an episode of *Extreme Makeover: Home Edition*," Mrs. Harris said, chuckling. "What do you have up your sleeve, Gabe?"

The store smelled like wood chips and fresh paint, one of Sadie's favorite aromas.

"Okay…open them!" Mr. Ludwig commanded.

The girls couldn't believe their eyes! The entire store had been painted a beautiful shade of purple. There were brand-new glass shelves from floor to ceiling, a crystal chandelier dangling from the ceiling, and in the very front, a giant display for Peace, Love, and Cupcakes.

"OMG!" Kylie gasped. "We get our own cupcake display?"

"Well, I thought having cupcakes at the Golden Spoon every week from the finalists for *Battle of the Bakers* would be a big draw for my customers." Mr. Ludwig winked.

"Dad, you did an amazing job!" Sadie exclaimed. The display looked like a giant cupcake with glass shelves from top to bottom.

"And you'll notice I did a peace sign on top…not a cherry," Mr. Harris added. "I know how Fiero feels about maraschino cherries."

Just then, Fiero, Carly, Jerry, *and* Mrs. Vanderwall stepped forward.

"You're here? You came?" Sadie said breathlessly. Dina, Cece, and Chloe were also there to celebrate.

"Well, zees gentleman said he has zee finest coop-cakes—so we had to taste for ourselves," Fiero said.

"And now that we see who makes them, I'm sure we won't be disappointed." Jerry smiled. "Right, Mrs. V?"

Sadie opened the box and handed her a Golden Caramel cupcake.

Mrs. Vanderwall took a lick…then another…then another.

"Mmmmm," she said. "Mmmmm….mmmmmmmm."

Kylie elbowed Sadie. "That's a definite 'I like it'!"

"You know, I discovered these girls," Mr. Ludwig began. "They owe it all to me."

"Here we go!" Jenna groaned.

"I have an incredible talent for finding culinary talent…"

"*Oui?* You like zee French macaroons?" Fiero interrupted.

"Do I like them? I love them!" Mr. Ludwig cried. "I could talk food for hours!"

"Then we'll be here a very, very long time," Mr. Harris whispered and tugged on Sadie's ponytail. "I can't understand a word that Fiero guy says!" He took Sadie's chin in his hand. "Did I mention how proud I am of you?"

"Yeah…a couple dozen times," Sadie said, blushing.

"We're proud of all of you," Jerry jumped in. "Which is why *Battle of the Bakers* decided to award you this." He handed Sadie a large white envelope.

"What is it?" she asked.

"Open it! Open it!" the girls screamed.

Inside was a check for $500—and a certificate that read, "In Special Recognition of *Battle of the Bakers'* Youngest Finalists: Peace, Love, and Cupcakes."

"OMG!" Kylie squealed. "So we're winners?"

"Apparently so," sniffed Mrs. Vanderwall. "I suppose even Michelangelo made a few mistakes now and then."

"That will cover the cost of the fondant printer we wanted," Lexi said. "Just think of all the awesome stuff we can make now!"

"With a display this size, I expect you to fill it weekly," Mr. Ludwig reminded them.

Sadie was thrilled—but not just over the check and the certificate and the crowd of customers gobbling up their cupcakes. She noticed that her mom and dad were not only getting along, they were holding hands in the corner of the Golden Spoon. Her mom was oohing and ahhing over her dad's handiwork, and they looked happy for the first time in a long time.

Kylie tossed her a cupcake, and Sadie caught it in one hand. She took a bite and savored the moment.

"Pretty good, huh?" Kylie asked her.

"Not just good…" Sadie smiled, licking the sticky caramel off her fingers. "Golden!"

Turn the page for three delicious
PLC recipes.

"No Business Like Snow Business" Snowball Coconut Cupcakes

Snowball Coconut Cupcakes

Makes 14

- ½ cup sweetened coconut flakes
  - + 2 tablespoons for garnish
- ½ cup butter, at room temperature
- ¾ cup sugar
- 1 ½ teaspoons vanilla extract
- 2 eggs
- 1 ½ cups all-purpose flour
- 1 ½ teaspoons baking powder
- ¼ teaspoon salt
- ½ cup coconut milk
- ½ cup sour cream

Directions

1. Preheat oven to 350°F. Place 14 cupcake liners in a cupcake pan.

2. Toast the coconut flakes on a cookie sheet for 10 minutes, or until golden brown.

3. In an electric mixer, cream butter and sugar until light and fluffy. Add in the vanilla extract and eggs, beating after each addition.

4. In a separate bowl, sift together the flour, baking powder, and salt. Add the dry mixture to the butter mixture, alternating with the coconut milk.

5. Beat in sour cream and toasted coconut flakes.

6. Fill cupcakes ¾ of the way. Bake for 16-18 minutes, or until a toothpick comes out clean.

7. Let cupcakes cool.

8. Once cupcakes are cooled, cut a circle about ½ inch deep out of the middle of the top of each cupcake.

9. Spoon Vanilla Meringue Frosting into the cut cupcakes.

10. Frost with Vanilla Meringue Frosting, and sprinkle with toasted coconut.

Vanilla Meringue Frosting

Makes 3 cups frosting

    4 large egg whites

    A pinch of salt

    1 cup of confectioners' sugar

    2 teaspoons vanilla

    ¼ teaspoon cream of tartar

Directions

1. Fill a pot half full with water. Simmer water.
2. Place a bowl on top of the pot, large enough so that it does not fall in or touch the water. Whisk all ingredients together in the bowl until the mixture is hot, about 2 minutes.
3. Take the mixture off the water and pour into an electric mixing bowl. Using the electric mixer, beat the hot egg mixture on high speed for 5 minutes, or until the mixture has cooled and stiff peaks have formed.

Golden Caramel Cupcakes with Caramel Buttercream Frosting

Golden Caramel Cupcakes
Makes 16

- ¾ cup unsalted butter, softened
- 1 cup sugar
- 3 eggs, separated
- ½ teaspoon vanilla extract
- 1 cup all-purpose flour
- ½ teaspoon baking powder
- ½ teaspoon baking soda
- ½ teaspoon salt
- ¾ cup buttermilk
- 1 cup Caramel Drizzle (recipe follows)
- 2 teaspoons gold sugar crystals

Directions

1. Preheat oven to 350°F. Line muffin tins with cupcake liners.

2. In a large bowl, cream butter and sugar until light and fluffy. Add egg yolks, one at a time, mixing until incorporated.

3. Add the vanilla, and mix until all ingredients are combined.

4. In a smaller bowl, sift together the flour, baking powder, baking soda, and salt. Add the dry mixture to the butter mixture, alternating with the buttermilk; end with the flour.

5. In a separate bowl, beat the egg whites until stiff peaks form. Fold into cake batter.

6. Pour 1 teaspoon of Caramel Drizzle into each liner. Add cupcake batter on top.

7. Fill cupcakes ¾ full. Bake 20 minutes, or until a toothpick comes out clean. Let cool in pan.

8. Allow cupcakes to cool. Once cool, fill a pastry bag or a squeeze bottle with half of the caramel. Push the tip into the cupcake and squeeze the caramel drizzle into the center.

9. Frost with Caramel Buttercream Frosting. Use a spoon to lightly drizzle on Caramel Drizzle, and sprinkle with gold sugar crystals.

Caramel Buttercream Frosting

Makes 3 cups frosting

    2 sticks unsalted butter, at room temperature

    4 cups confectioners' sugar

    A pinch of salt

    1 tablespoon vanilla extract

    1 tablespoon milk

    3 tablespoons Caramel Drizzle

Directions

1. Beat the butter until smooth.
2. Add confectioners' sugar and salt. Beat until most of the sugar is moistened, scraping down the sides of the bowl once or twice.
3. When the mixture is fully combined, add vanilla, milk, and Caramel Drizzle.
4. Increase speed and beat until light and fluffy, about 4 minutes.

Caramel Drizzle

Note: If making Caramel Drizzle, please have adult supervision and use caution when melting sugar. You can' also substitute with a jar of store-bought caramel sauce.

Makes 1 cup Caramel Drizzle

1 cup sugar

6 tablespoons butter

½ cup heavy cream

Directions

1. Heat sugar on medium-high heat in a medium-sized sauce pan. As the sugar begins to melt, constantly stir with a wooden spoon.

2. Stop stirring as soon as the sugar begins to boil. Once all of the sugar is melted, add the butter and whisk until all the butter is melted.

3. After the butter has melted, take the mixture off the heat. Count to five and very slowly add the heavy cream to the pot, stirring constantly. At this time, the mixture will dramatically increase.

4. At this point, the caramel will be extremely hot. Let cool until room temperature and refrigerate to thicken.

"The Perfect Pair" Chocolate Chili Cupcakes with Cream Cheese Frosting

Chocolate Chili Cupcakes
Makes 12

- 1 cup all-purpose flour
- ½ cup cocoa powder
- 1 cup sugar
- 1 teaspoon baking soda
- 1 teaspoon baking powder
- ½ teaspoon salt
- ¼ teaspoon cayenne pepper
- 1 egg
- ½ cup milk
- ¼ cup vegetable oil
- ½ teaspoon vanilla
- ½ cup warm water
- 2 tablespoons cocoa powder, for dusting

Directions

1. Preheat oven to 350°F. Line the muffin pan.
2. Mix together flour, cocoa powder, sugar, baking soda, baking powder, salt, and cayenne pepper.
3. Add the eggs, milk, oil, vanilla, and warm water. Mix until smooth and combined.
4. Divide batter evenly among the cups, filling each ¾ full.
5. Bake until a toothpick comes out clean, about 15 minutes.
6. Cool cupcakes and frost with Cream Cheese Frosting.
7. Lightly sift cocoa powder on top.

Cream Cheese Frosting

Makes 2 cups frosting

4 tablespoons unsalted butter at room temperature

1 cup cream cheese

4 cups of confectioners' sugar

2 teaspoons vanilla

Directions

1. Beat the butter and cream cheese until smooth.
2. Add confectioners' sugar and salt. Beat until most of the sugar is moistened, scraping down the sides of the bowl once or twice.

3. When the mixture is fully combined, add vanilla.
4. Increase speed and beat until light and fluffy, about 4 minutes.

Recipes developed by Jessi Walter, Founder and Chief Bud at Taste Buds Kitchen (www.tastebudskitchen.com).

Carrie's Tips for Throwing Your Own Cupcake Challenge!

It's a lot of fun to stage a baking battle in your own kitchen. I've done it tons of times with friends—and the best part is eating whatever you make! Everyone's a winner!

1. Divide your friends into two or three teams—and pick a name for your teams. For example, "Sweet Sensations" or "Cupcake Queens." I like to make a poster with our team name on it. It puts you in the mood!

2. Pick older members of your family—like your mom, dad, or siblings—to be the judges. (Younger ones can help, too.) The adults can also help you put cupcakes in the oven and take them out.

3. Come up with a theme for the cupcake battle. I've done lots of different themes, like "Pirates and Princesses," "Easter Eggs," and "Haunted Halloween." I've even done one to celebrate the royal wedding in England!

Any occasion or idea is a great one! I decide ahead of time so I can provide my friends with cupcake decorations and wrappers that match the theme.

4. Set the timer for *exactly* 60 minutes. The cupcakes should take about 20 minutes to bake, which leaves you enough time to mix, cool, decorate, and display your cupcakes. Pick one flavor to bake for both teams (unless you have two mixers and can make two flavors).

5. Your team gets to decide how they will color, fill, and frost the cupcakes. Here's how you set yourself apart from the competition! For Halloween, we made gross green frosting ooze out of a chocolate cupcake. Then we put gummy spiders on top. Make sure each team has a lot of choices: fill small cups with different types of candies, sprinkles, and chips. You can also provide food coloring (to dye your cupcake batter) and fondant (to make small figures or decorations).

6. Make sure the judge sets a timer and tells you every 5 to 10 minutes how much time is remaining. It's a lot of fun when you know the clock is ticking down…that makes it even more exciting and like a real cupcake battle.

7. After you have frosted your cupcakes, display them creatively. I have a cupcake tower so I love to stack

mine high. You could also serve them in a circle, on a silver platter, with bows around the wrapper, any way you think will impress the judges!

8. Finally, ask your judges to rate the cupcakes on taste, decoration, and theme. I like to give the winner a cupcake-themed prize, like some pretty cupcake wrappers or a cupcake charm. Congrats!

For more cupcake news, reviews, recipes, and tips, check out Carrie's website: www.carriescupcakecritique .shutterfly.com and Facebook page: www.facebook.com/ PLCCupcakeClub. You can also email her at carrieplcclub@ aol.com.

Acknowledgments

Hugs and sprinkles go out to:

Our loving family: the Kahns, Berks, and Saperstones. (Jason, when are you making the movie version?)

Our *amazing* recipe developer, Jessi Walter of Taste Buds. (Now a Mrs.! Congrats!)

Our PS 6 family, especially Ms. Fontana, Ms. Levenherz, and Ms. Errico.

Carrie's BFFs: Jaimie Ludwig and Darby Dutter—what would I do without you two?

The BAE Level 3 girls, especially Julia Applebaum and Alexa Malone (stretch, girls!); and PS 6 pals Delaney Hannon, Abby Johnson, Ava Nobandegani, Brynn and Dale Heller.

Carrie's Camp Hillard crew: Julia Goldberg, Reina McNutt, Rebecca Pomerantz, Jessica Roth, Sara Binday, Allison Lax, and Erin Donahue. *Grease* is the word! And Gabby Borenstein—my fave Hillard counselor forever!

Sheryl's supporting cast: Holly Russell, Kathy Passero, Stacy Polsky, Pam Kaplan, Michele Alfano, and Debbie Skolnik.

The cupcake experts who have been so supportive of *Carrie's Cupcake Critique*: Katherine Kallinis and Sophie LaMontagne of *DC Cupcakes*; *Cake Boss* Buddy Valastro; Doron Petersan of Sticky Fingers, and Rachel Kramer Bussel and Nichelle Stephens of the *Cupcakes Take the Cake* blogspot.

The folks at Sourcebooks Jabberwocky—we couldn't ask for a better team to work with! Steve Geck, Derry Wilkens, Leah Hultenschmidt, Aubrey Poole, Helen Nam, and Jillian Bergsma.

Illustrator extraordinaire Julia Denos for bringing the PLC characters to life on every cover.

Our agents at the Literary Group: Frank Weimann, Katherine Latshaw, and Elyse Tanzillo.

About the Authors

Photo by Heidi Green

New York Times bestselling co-author of *Soul Surfer*, Sheryl Berk was the founding editor-in-chief of *Life & Style Weekly* as well as a contributor to *InStyle*, *Martha Stewart*, and other publications. She has written dozens of books with celebrities including Britney Spears, Jenna Ushkowitz, and Zendaya. Her 10-year-old daughter, Carrie Berk, a cupcake connoisseur and blogger, cooked up the idea for The Cupcake Club series while in second grade. Together, they have invented dozens of crazy cupcake recipes in their NYC kitchen (can you say "Purple Velvet"?) and have the frosting stains on the ceiling to prove it. They love writing together and have many more adventures in store for the PLC girls!